D1484419

*[for other titles and publications please see from page 250]*

# THE SON OF GOD
# AND SEED OF DAVID

# THE
# SON OF GOD
## AND
# SEED OF DAVID

*The Apostolic Foundation of the Christian Church*

*Volume Four*

JOHN METCALFE

JOHN METCALFE PUBLISHING TRUST

Tylers Green Chapel · Penn · Buckinghamshire

John Metcalfe Publishing Trust
Penn, Buckinghamshire

—

First published 1979

—

Copyright John Metcalfe Publishing Trust, 1979
All rights reserved

—

ISBN  0 9506366 1 4

—

Printed and handmade in England
by John Metcalfe Publishing Trust
Tylers Green Chapel
Penn
Buckinghamshire

—

*Price £1.10*

# A REVIEW
## by Dr. David Hughes

This latest book by John Metcalfe is a further volume in the major work entitled 'The Apostolic Foundation of the Christian Church'.

As with the earlier volumes, the reader feels that this man has kept company with Christ and his holy apostles, and is sent directly to our age to expose the glaring disparity between modern Christianity and theirs, to root out and to pull down, to destroy and to throw down, thenceforward to build up and to plant.

Dealing with the irreducible summary of the apostolic gospel in Romans 1:3-4, attention is first drawn to truths in it which the modern gospel never mentions, much less considers foundational. The author, opening and alleging that Jesus Christ is and ever was THE SON OF GOD, brings proof after proof and furnishes scripture upon scripture, with overwhelming effect. Who can withstand this avalanche of undeniable evidence?

This greatest of subjects, this most profound of all mysteries, is handled with reverence and with outstanding perception.

From plumbing such depths, the book now soars in consideration of THE SEED OF DAVID. We are admonished by Paul not to forget that 'Jesus Christ came of the seed of David according to my gospel.' But why is this so pivotal? What is meant precisely by 'the seed'? And why 'of David'? With prophetic insight the author expounds these crucial verities.

A wealth of divine enlightenment appears. Reaching to magnificence, we now behold David the man, David the heir, and David the king. This flows, page after page, seraphic and sublime. Passages soar in eloquence; heights are scaled as the truth is unfolded with piercing clarity.

Christ's reign is seen to be twofold: spiritually at present in the saints, and absolutely in the world to come. The spiritual conflict for world dominion will be decisively resolved. Here the book reaches a crescendo as it appears just how near that day we are, as the fast-moving events of the twentieth century are prophetically and penetratingly analysed.

In conclusion, one's summary upon laying down *The Son of God and Seed of David* is this:   Here is doctrine on fire.

31454

*David Hughes, B.Sc., M.B., Ch.B.*

# CONTENTS

# CONTENT

# THE
# SON OF GOD
## AND
# SEED OF DAVID

Paul, a servant of Jesus Christ, called to be an
apostle, separated unto the gospel of God ....
   (which he had promised afore by his
   prophets in the holy scriptures)
.... Concerning his Son Jesus Christ our Lord,
which was made of the seed of David
according to the flesh;
And declared to be the Son of God with
power, according to the spirit of holiness, by
the resurrection from the dead.

*Romans 1:1-4.*

IN THESE opening verses of the epistle to the saints at
Rome Paul summarises the gospel. One thing stands out
above everything else:

## THE GOSPEL IS CONCERNED EXCLUSIVELY
## WITH THE SON OF GOD.

1

'Concerning his Son.' The gospel concerns God's Son. That is, the person of Christ: 'Jesus Christ our Lord'. Not until the third chapter of this epistle do we get to the work of Christ. In the apostolic gospel the person precedes the work and that is how it is preached. This is what is presented to faith and must be believed to be saved.

The cross is in chapter three but the Crucified is in chapter one. The blood of propitiation is in 3:25 but the Propitiatory himself is in 1:3-4. The gospel does not start with the work of Christ, it starts with the Worker, Christ himself. Apostolic preaching does not commence with what the Son of God has done. It commences with whom he is: it declares his Person.

This agrees with the revelation of the person and work of the Holy Ghost in John chapters fourteen to sixteen.

Having prophesied of the sending and coming of the Comforter to his own, Jesus goes on to declare what he is sent for and what he comes to do. This appears in John 15:26. Jesus is speaking of the coming of the Spirit of truth and he says, He shall testify of me. That first. That is, testify of the person of Christ first. 'Testify of me.'

This is seen again in John 16:14, He shall glorify me. But now the work proceeds further, and the way in which the Lord Jesus is glorified is extended: For he shall receive of mine, and shall show it unto you. Christ is glorified by the Spirit doing that.

What is glorified now is not only his person, it is what proceeds from his person, what that person does. It is his work. 'He shall take of mine.' That is, the work of Christ. That is the second thing the Spirit takes and shows for the

2

glory of Christ. Not now the person that he is, but the things which he has done. That is what the Spirit of truth takes, secondly, and shows to his own. 'Show it unto you.' The work of Christ.

This prophecy of Jesus to and through the apostles is seen to come to pass with the apostle Paul in the epistle to the Romans. The Holy Ghost, the Comforter, acting as the Spirit of truth, leads Paul into all truth so as to set forth the gospel in its divine and spiritual order. And this is to glorify the person of Christ first, chapter one; so leading on to the glorious work of Christ next, beginning at the third chapter.

Thus the apostolic doctrine secures the truth of what was done at Calvary only after the person that did the work is esteemed aright. As the Son of God is set before the eye of faith, so he is wonderfully magnified and glorified, being understood and valued according to the revelation of God and the Father.

That is how the Father reveals the Son. As one who must be honoured — cherished — according to truth. This is not what he has done or does for you: it is what he is in himself. His person. This is how the gospel puts things in their own proper order according to the revelation of the Spirit of God. But a moment of reflection will confirm that it must be so. Only because of the worth and value of the Lord's unique being, could the perfection of his wonderful work have the character that it does.

First and foremost it is not a question of truths about him. He is himself the truth and that is what needs to be seen and appreciated. He is the primary subject of God's gospel. Therefore every gospel truth declaring what he has done, is doing, or will do, takes its place in relation to his person as revealed. Truths are not detached to form a distinct creed, theology or philosophy. There is one truth and he is it. That is why the gospel is called, The doctrine of Christ.

The value of Jesus' work depends entirely upon the greatness and virtue of his person. Therefore the real worth of any professed faith in his sacrifice at Calvary must be weighed in the balance of what is believed about his person. These two things can never be separated. Otherwise only a fragment of the gospel would be believed, not the gospel itself.

The reality of the person of the Son of God is the essence of the gospel giving radiance and character to all that is declared about his deeds. The gospel teaches the truth about the person of the Son, and commands the faithful willingly and gladly to submit to the obedience of the faith among all nations. This is the faith that the apostles taught in the name of the Father, and of the Son, and of the Holy Ghost. Such authority. How could anybody casting himself upon this gospel fail to be saved?

Father, Son and Holy Ghost reveal from heaven a noble, magnificent evangel: the gospel of God concerning his Son. This revelation declares that the way to honour and love the Lord Jesus is to believe the gospel. To hear and understand just who it is that we are to glorify by believing upon him.

Essentially God declares five things about the person of his Son here at the beginning of the gospel.

4

1. THAT HE WAS THE SON OF GOD.

2. THAT HE 'WAS MADE' ACCORDING TO THE FLESH.

3. THAT HE 'WAS MADE' OF THE SEED OF DAVID.

4. THAT HE 'IS DECLARED' ACCORDING TO THE SPIRIT.

5. THAT HE 'IS DECLARED' BY THE RESURRECTION.

It is with the first three of these headings that the present volume is concerned. As 'The Apostolic Foundation of the Christian Church' continues as a whole, so the truth concerned in the fourth and fifth headings must be unfolded. At present, for the sake of context, I note the scope of Romans 1:3-4. However, only the third verse demands our attention in this volume.

He who hears, understands, and believes this fivefold testimony from the heart, is one who of a truth believes on the name of the only begotten Son of God. Here is one who believes the gospel.

Moreover in this place God gives his Son two names for the confession of faith. The first is in verse three, the second in verse four.

1. JESUS CHRIST OUR LORD.

Not just Jesus, you see. He was that, in the humiliation of his life throughout the

5

gospels. But now his work on earth is done and done to perfection. Now he is crowned with glory and honour and appropriately named. Whoso fails so to name him cannot truly glorify him.

And it is 'our' Lord. It is plural. One body is seen under this Head. Here are those who mortify themselves to take their place under the Lord's headship in one Spirit with their brethren as subject to the apostles' doctrine. 'Our' Lord.

The second name follows in verse four:

## 2. THE SON OF GOD.

Who knows the power that is in the truth of this name? The pre-existence of it? The eternity of it? The manifestation of it? The declaration of it? The obedience to it? What a name this is and what a spiritual declaration: 'The Son of God'.

He who knows and feels these things and confesses them, verily such an one is a believer indeed, sound in the apostles' fellowship, walking in the Spirit, and holding the unity of one body. This is to be of the faithful. This is to hold fast the faith.

Faith is not something we induce within ourselves. It is created by The Faith; that is, by the objective truth of the gospel. The response of the heart and confession of the mouth to that, is called our faith. But the faith is another thing. We have faith when we believe and confess The Faith. The Faith is what we believe; our faith is our believing it.

Faith comes by hearing and hearing by the word of God. That word is objective. And that word of the gospel is exclusively about Christ. Not man at all. Not systematic creeds. It is all about the Son of God and it commences by declaring his person.

The scriptures of the Old Testament confirm this, verse two: 'Which he had promised afore by his prophets in the holy scriptures.'

First, this is an appeal to antiquity. The promise of the gospel did not commence with this epistle. No, nor even with the Advent in the gospels. God's commencement was in the beginning of Genesis. And from the beginning God by his holy prophets assures us of the verity of our faith now, by the long continued prophecies, witness, types, shadows, descriptions, figures and promises then.

This true gospel is no innovation. It was promised from the foundation of the world. Therefore what the apostle is about to declare to us is solid as it is rock; founded in the holy mountains.

Second, the scriptures of the Old Testament — far from being outmoded and irrelevant at the present time — actually teach this selfsame gospel of God. Admittedly, a divine discernment is needed to distinguish between things that differ when interpreting the gospel from the Old Testament.

Nevertheless 'Beginning at Moses and all the prophets, Jesus expounded unto them in all the scriptures the things concerning himself,' Luke 24:27. And again, 'All things' saith Jesus 'must be fulfilled which were written in the law of Moses, and in the prophets, and in the psalms, concerning me,' Luke 24:44.

Agreed, spiritual discrimination is required to interpret aright. However it is still true that the Old Testament scriptures not only promise the gospel but they are full of its teaching. As to how we may obtain such a discrimination, this follows, Luke 24:45 'Then opened he their understanding, that they might understand the scriptures.'

Once understood, these wonderful books reveal a multitude of promises of the gospel of God concerning his Son and reveal it from the very first words of the Bible. Not only so, but in a great variety of ways, the same Old Testament scriptures themselves actually manifest glimpses of the gospel in ways that, often, can scarcely be surpassed for clarity of vision even in the New Testament.

However, in Romans our attention is drawn actually to the sole apostolically authorised, divinely inspired, and infallibly given exposition of the doctrine of the gospel. The apostolic testimony; as such, exclusively found within the record of the New Testament. Particularly is this true of Paul's epistle to the Romans. Here the beginning of the gospel is opened at length as the general subject of the epistle. Nevertheless within that narrative are to be found especially lucid and pithy summaries and definitions of the whole.

And nowhere in this epistle is the gospel reduced to such comprehensive terms — condensed to the barest essentials;

the iron rations; the irreducible criteria of definition — as in this succinct résumé in chapter one verses three and four. Everything is refined down to the absolute. Miss a word, even a hint, and the verses would no longer summarise the whole gospel. Here is found the ultimate in reduction; here the *sine qua non* of analysis; it is *the* summary of the gospel. Everything is found: but found only in its essence. And this that we should all learn and memorise.

In this definition of the gospel of God concerning his Son — chapter one verses three and four — we have shown that the apostle reveals five consecutive things about the person of the Son of God. Our concern in this volume is to expound the first three, found within the third verse.

Of these three, the opening statement is so obvious that it would be easy to overlook it or merge it with the next. Easy, but entirely wrong. The first and great definitive gospel revelation about the Lord Jesus is this:

# I

# THAT HE WAS THE SON OF GOD

# The Son of God

CONSIDER THIS expression: 'His Son, Jesus Christ our Lord, which was made of the seed of David according to the flesh.'

That the Son of God 'was made' of the seed of David according to the flesh, clearly shows his pre-existence.

To be so made, he himself must have been in existence for the subsequent 'making' to have happened to him. The 'he' that was made, was a 'he' existent before the making took place. It must be so. The Son of God who 'was', thereafter 'was made'.

It is not that he was made the Son of God. It is that the Son of God was made 'according to the flesh'. If so, prior to this 'making' his being was in no way 'according to the flesh'. Nevertheless it was existent. Then existent in a form entirely spiritual.

Now see what we are being taught.

We are instructed that the Son of God 'which was', was *before*. Before being so made, he was. Then his pre-existence is seen.

But more. His pre-existence in the name of Son. That is what the holy apostle is saying. 'His Son ... which was made.' Therefore he was the Son before being so made.

Not simply pre-existent, which must follow. But pre-existent in the name and nature of Son. Had he not intended us to understand this, the apostle would not have used the language that he does. The conclusion of pre-existence, and that in the relationship of Son is inescapable.

11

From which follows of necessity the commensurate existence of his Father. And it is not too much to add from this place, united in one Spirit. Nor to say, that we glimpse the revelation of the deity in Father, Son and Holy Ghost.

The Son of God 'which was', was without beginning. The self-existent one. The I AM. But at a certain point in time the I AM of eternity 'was made' of the seed of David according to the flesh. It is the Son of God who was so made. Then his everlasting deity is predicated. And if so everlasting deity revealed in the relationship of Father, Son and Holy Ghost.

All that 'which was' quietly leads us to this response. Certainly it is inferential: but it is also unquestionable. It requires of us our perceptive faith and illuminated belief.

Not our understanding. That is why it is not explained. Because this mystery of godliness is inexplicable. It cannot be rationalised. It is a mystery, not to be reasoned about.

God has revealed the truth in his Son by what has happened to his Son. We are to receive it with meekness, and meekly to receive all of it; with humility believe it, and humbly to believe all of it. Because it is the gospel of God concerning his Son.

Let no man attempt to rationalise it, for reason is unequal to the task. Let none attempt to grasp it intellectually, for the deity lies beyond all human intelligence to grasp. It is essential with this most profound of all mysteries, this most absolute of all truths, that man curb his reason, restrain his intellect, and submit to revelation. It is his to worship. Not to question.

This requires the admission of finiteness in the face of infinity, mortality in the face of eternity, fragility in the face of immutability, vanity in the face of the absolute, fear before the presence of the great God, the Maker of heaven and earth.

But these are things man in his nature is loath to admit and reluctant to yield. Man impudently challenges the knowledge of the Father and the Son, disobeying and despising the revelation of the gospel.

The person of the Son of God has been continually attacked, and is being attacked. Not only overtly, covertly also. Not only by blatant blasphemy, also by feigned words. Not only by aggression, also by treacherously false love. Not only by opposing him but also by ignoring him. Not only by atheism, but also by agnosticism.

This is not a day for open animosity towards the Son of God. It is a day for soft dissolution, with which there is much profession of love. Still for all the current blandishments of love and peace, life and liberty, fellowship and reconciliation, behind this fair show lies enough corrupt error against the Son, or at least enough wilfully ignoring and despising the truth about him, enough, I say, to damn the soul beneath the charge of unbelief.

It must be appreciated that no doctrine at all is as disobedient to the faith as all false doctrine. That alliance with those who disobey the faith is as disobedient — for those personally obeying it — as if one disobeyed oneself. All these things must be borne in mind.

However, when every hidden thing is brought to light, and all cloaks are ripped aside, it will be discovered that

13

attacks upon the Son of God are now, just as they have always been, of four kinds:

- ☐ They attack his deity.

- ☐ They attack his eternal relationship with the Father.

- ☐ They attack his humanity.

- ☐ They attack the relationship of his humanity with his deity.

Apropos of this, let me say that

## 1. THE DEITY OF THE SON IS REVEALED IN AT LEAST FIVE WAYS.

*(i) Firstly, By direct references.*

As to the deity of the Son, the most famous of a great multitude of passages are, for example:

John 1:1, In the beginning was the Word, and the Word was with God, and the Word was God. Isaiah 9:6, His name shall be called the mighty God. Philippians 2:6, Who, being in the form of God, thought it not robbery to be equal with God. I Timothy 3:16, God was manifest in the flesh. I John 5:20, This is the true God, and eternal life. Matthew 1:23, A virgin shall be with child, and shall bring forth a son, and they shall call his name Emmanuel, which being interpreted is, God with us. John 10:30, I and my Father are one.

*(ii) Secondly, By personal testimony.*

For example, that of God the Father to the Son.

Hebrews 1:8, Unto the Son he saith, Thy throne, O God, is for ever and ever. Again in Hebrews 1, the Father, God, addresses the Son, God: Therefore God, thy God hath anointed thee.

Once more in Hebrews 1, God the Father saith to the Son: Thou, Lord, in the beginning hast laid the foundation of the earth; and the heavens are the works of thine hands. Yet Genesis 1 assures us: In the beginning God created the heaven and the earth. And the heavens were the works of his hands.

For example, the testimony of angels to the Son.

Revelation 5:11-12, And I heard the voice of many angels, and the number of them was ten thousand times ten thousand, and thousands of thousands, saying with a loud voice, Worthy is the Lamb that was slain to receive power, and riches, and wisdom, and strength, and honour, and glory, and blessing.

A sevenfold plurality due to the deity alone given by angels to the Son only, even as he sits on the Father's throne in heaven.

As it is written, Let all the angels of God worship him. But, Thou shalt worship the Lord thy God, and him only shalt thou serve. Clearly showing angelic testimony to the deity of the Son.

For example, the testimony of men to the Son.

## The Son of God

First, the fathers.

Enoch prophesied of the second coming of the Son to judgment — the prerogative of the deity — well before the flood, Genesis 5 and Jude verse 14. Melchizedek appeared as the pre-existent Son of God well before the existence of Israel, Genesis 14. Abraham rejoiced to see the Son in his day, lowering himself to the ground and worshipping. Moreover Jacob saw God face to face and worshipped at Peniel. And seventy elders of Israel saw Jehovah at Sinai. Isaiah beheld his glory. Also, Daniel saw God and lived.

Yet no man hath seen God — that is, in terms of the Father exclusively — at any time, insists John 1:18. But the only begotten Son which is in the bosom of the Father, he hath declared him. Then, it was the Son whom the patriarchs saw and worshipped. If so, they confessed his divinity.

Second, the prophets.

Micah saw the Son and observed that his goings were from everlasting. His name is Jehovah our righteousness, Jeremiah assures Israel. Saith God by Isaiah the prophet, Unto me every knee shall bow; but Paul the apostle interprets that it is to the Son that every knee shall bow: a thing impossible were Isaiah and Paul not speaking of the Son as God, one and the same. Zechariah calls Christ the Branch; but the name of the Branch is Jehovah.

Third, the apostles.

Saith even the doubter, My Lord and my God. Saith Saul — in a vision — to Jesus, Who art thou, Lord? But to the Jews the Lord was Jehovah. Saith the Jews, He makes himself equal with God; saith Paul, He is equal with God. The four and twenty elders, mystical rulers of all the Israel of God and the whole church of God, say to the Son, Thou art worthy, O Lord, for thou hast created all things, and for thy pleasure they are and were created. Saith the Hebrews, He is the brightness of God's glory, and the express image of his person.

But saith God, My glory will I not give to another. Neither has he, for the Son is God: that is where the glory of God properly belongs: in the deity.

Another example of personal testimony to the Son's deity is seen in the types.

To name but a few, the mercy seat was God's throne. Gold was its substance, showing God and his throne were inseparable, for gold was the figure of the reflective glory of God himself. But Romans 3 and Hebrews 9 tell us that the Son is actually the one whom the mercy seat typified.

The manna was the figure of the bread of God from heaven, but John tells us God himself is that manna, and that the Son of God is the true bread from heaven.

Saith Christ of the water in the wilderness, the Rock which followed them, the wells of salvation, the floods upon the dry ground: 'If any man thirst, let him come unto me and drink.' This utterance fulfilled those scriptural types: Christ is the water. But that is a divine prerogative, for saith God almighty, I am the fountain of living waters. Well, saith Christ, come unto me and drink.

But to continue; we are proposing that the deity of the Son is revealed in at least five ways.

*(iii) Then, thirdly, By his possessing the attributes and functions of deity.*

The Son does what the Father did: My Father worketh hitherto, and I work. As the Father sent me so send I you. The Son can do nothing but what he seeth the Father do; but that, he can do. Then who is he?

As the Father raiseth the dead and quickeneth: even so the Son quickeneth whom he will. All men should honour the Son as they honour the Father. And how do they honour the Father? As God, of course.

He that hath seen me hath seen the Father. I speak that which I have seen with my Father. I do the works of my Father. I am in the Father and the Father in me. Many works have I shown from my Father.

Said John, Jesus knew all things. All things?

Said the Pharisees, Who can forgive sins but God only? Jesus said, Son, thy sins be forgiven thee. And they were.

Philip said, Show us the Father. Jesus replied, Have I been so long time with you, and yet hast thou not known me, Philip?

Without him was not anything made that was made. That is the creation. As a vesture thou shalt fold them up. That is the conflagration. Meantime there is the judgment: The Father hath given all judgment to the Son. But nothing is more certain than that the Eternal reserves to himself alone the exclusive right to judge the world.

But the Son and the Father are one. He is the Eternal.

The Son is 'without beginning of days nor end of life.' Indeed, Thy throne, O God, is for ever and ever. I AM, he says seven times over, the exclusive name of Jehovah God. Then it indicates the divine perfection of the Son's eternity.

### (iv) Fourthly, By his receiving worship.

The Son receives equal worship with the Father: That all men should honour the Son even as they honour the Father. Hence he saith, Ye believe in God: believe also in me. That is, they believed in God known — though veiled — as Jehovah in the Old Testament; in that manner of belief, 'Also in me.' But, Thou shalt worship the Lord thy God and him only shalt thou serve. Nevertheless, Also in me.

Indeed, men worshipped the Son. Heaven worships the Son. Angels worshipped the Son.

God the Father commands all heaven, every angel, regarding the Son: Let all the angels of God worship him. And since obedience to his commandments is certain then the whole angelic host, all the redeemed, the entire celestial sphere does in fact worship the Son upon the throne of God in glory; there is but one conclusion: He is divine, the eternal God, in his own person.

### (v) Fifthly, By the necessity of redemption.

Because of the lowly servitude and mean exterior taken by the Son of God in the vast stoop which he made for us men and our salvation we are not through this to be deceived by appearances. Of necessity in his incarnation as

19

a poor and helpless babe the Son laid aside the radiant appearance, the ineffable glory, all the honour, dignity and visible manifestation emanating from his divine nature: all this was put aside, it was hidden. But the little babe appeared.

For the Son was thus manifest in the flesh so as to give all glory and honour to the Father. In redemption the Son takes such a lowly place, and the Holy Spirit even a lowlier, that the deity is explicitly glorified, honoured and made known only in God and the Father.

Such is the stoop of grace, such is the condescension of the incarnation, such is his love for us in taking the place of man.

But we are not by this to be deceived by the exterior appearance. For if redemption necessitated his humiliation as man, it also necessitated, uniquely, *his* humiliation as man. And here appearances seem to the contrary.

For were not that unrevealed deity true of him in his humiliation on earth, redemption would have been impossible. Redemption necessitated that the Redeemer must be divine. Salvation absolutely required deity of the Saviour.

His divinity — though its glorious manifestation be laid aside, hidden from view — was always and is always true of his innate being; no matter how profound his humiliation in manhood, even at the moment of death, even the death of the cross.

And it was the worth of his deity that gave an incalculably multiplied value to his manhood. His impeccable humanity gave him the absolute right to stand as the perfect substitute for the sinner. Man for man.

But his divine nature and person enhanced that humanity and gave a value to his manhood beyond all calculation, extending the virtue of that substitution to a great multitude which no man can number, yea, even to as many as the Lord our God shall call.

In the offering up of his spotless humanity at Calvary, as the substitute of sinful men, that manhood of his was as it were cradled within the hands of his deity. Just as the shittim wood of the Ark was cradled in the gold with which it was overlaid.

In the incarnation the Son of God united with his divine nature that impeccable human nature created within the womb of the virgin Mary; and at the cross he offered up that humanity a spotless sacrifice to God on behalf of all those whom he came to redeem.

But in the nature of the *he* who did so, that humanity was invested with a worth and uniqueness far beyond one sacrifice for one sinner. The Son was able to give an absoluteness to the sacrifice, a divinity to the offering, an eternity to its duration, an infinity of satisfaction to God and the Father on behalf of so vast a number, that what happened so far exceeded the bare appearance of the crucifixion as heaven is high above the earth.

Thus his sacrifice became of sufficient substitutionary worth for so great a multitude, because his humanity was as it were offered upon the altar of his deity. His divine nature extended the effects of his perfect human offering, and infinitely enhanced its value, not only to be for one but for all; not only to be once for all but once for all for ever; for eternity, for infinity; but absolutely, absolutely satisfactory to the divine nature.

Thus he is Jacob's ladder in his nature and in his sacrifice: he reaches up to Almighty God and reaches down to the Israel of God.

He is the one mediator, but one between God and men, because he unites both in his singular person, and reconciles each in his unique sacrifice.

Thus he is the one priest, able to speak to men for God, and to God for men, bringing in one sacrifice once for ever satisfying the conscience of men, the justice of the law and the righteousness of God.

So he accomplishes redemption and thus he achieves salvation because of the uniqueness of his person: thence the distinctiveness of his sacrifice.

Wherefore it follows from this alone — accomplished redemption — that here we see abundantly demonstrated the pre-existent, everlasting deity of him who by himself — by himself, mark it — purged our sins, and is sat down on the right hand of the Majesty on high, from henceforth expecting till all his enemies be made his footstool.

From the preceding five points it is clear that the deity of the Son is revealed. It is plain that he who was 'made of the seed of David according to the flesh' existed, or pre-existed, before being so made. And this the words imply.

Moreover that he did so in the form of God. He existed from eternity possessed of his own everlasting deity. And hence we predicate the first and great truth about the person of the Son of God.

★

However, further to implying his deity, the statement THAT HE WAS THE SON OF GOD proposes another pre-eminent truth. It is this:

## 2. THE RELATIONSHIP OF SON WITH THE FATHER IS ETERNAL.

That is, the everlasting deity of the Eternal God stands in the mystery — holy, unapproachable and inexplicable — of three distinct divine persons, Father, Son and Holy Ghost, ever subsisting in absolute spiritual union in the one divine essence that is God.

This mystery is never explained in the Bible. It is never expounded in doctrine. Never reasoned or argued about in the New Testament. It is not often mentioned, but where it is, it is with sublime assurance; unquestioned, unprobed, the mystery is taken for granted.

It is the mystery that stands in spiritual and divine Being. It is not discerned by considering God in and of himself. It is a mystery revealed in the Son and only discerned aright when the Son is made known within. 'He that hath seen me hath seen the Father.'

This mystery of the being of God absolutely defies created understanding, whether seraphic, angelic or human. If the infinity of space eludes comprehension: if the eternity of duration stuns the imagination: if the indestructibility of matter makes the mind to fail: if men retreat from things too high for them, things possessed of an absoluteness beyond, quite beyond, human capacity: then what of the nature of God himself?

One will ask, These things being so, then why do you make statements about the nature of God?

But it is God that has made the statements which we repeat. It is God who gave his only begotten Son, sending him into the world. It is God whose purpose is so great in his Son. It is God who, having redeemed a people by the Son of his love, justified them by his blood, called them by his grace, gathered them under the sound of the apostolic gospel, filled them with his Spirit, now makes himself known to them in a mystery.

In experience then, within, they become the temple of the Holy Ghost. They become the body of Christ. They become the house of God and the Father. By sweet experience they are consciously filled with what they could never, can never, and never will explain: the fulness of God. About this, they can but repeat the statements that he himself has made, thereafter laying their hands upon their mouths.

There is given to them from God out of heaven what they could never achieve on earth by themselves: the spiritual knowledge of God, Father, Son, and Holy Ghost. But this knowledge they will never fail both to maintain and defend.

They cannot explain it. In any event it is inexplicable. But believing the gospel, receiving the Spirit, has brought about the mystery unknown. Experiencing together in unity the indwelling of Father, Son and Holy Ghost, they are consciously aware of one God, and withal, of three persons in the one indivisible Godhead.

This awareness they hear of and discover in the apostles' doctrine. Stated: not explained. This consciousness they see has before been shared by the church of which they read in the Bible. It is never argued. It is stated, and it is implied.

One God in three persons; three persons in one God; known in the experience of the saints.

The Spirit having subjected himself to glorify the Son. The Son having taken a subject place to the glory of the Father. The Son and the Spirit ascribing deity in and to God and the Father. The Spirit leading the saints to cry, 'Abba, Father.' The Son uniting the saints with himself in God and the Father.

No — not explained — simply asserted. No — not explicable — only experienced. No — not indoctrinated — but clearly written. But as called, separated, gathered and united under the gospel, brethren are conscious of the love of God, Father, Son, and Holy Ghost, shed abroad in their hearts by the Holy Ghost given unto them.

Of necessity the explanation must defy human reason, and the comprehension of the mystery must pass all understanding. Nevertheless the reality is the experience of the humble and united saints walking together in the truth of the gospel, the fear of God, and the comfort of the Holy Ghost.

But worldly men are enraged to find something beyond their ability. The carnal mind feels challenged to attempt the explanation.

Neither can hirelings bear to have their lack of experience discovered. Those had in great reputation find a need to enhance their standing. And hence many stumble on the rock and fall into great and grievous errors at this stone of offence.

Therefore we are bound to assert the truth: *the relationship of the Father and the Son is an eternal relationship in the deity.*

Romans 1:3 informs us that the gospel of God concerns his Son. He was the one who was 'made of the seed of David according to the flesh.' He was made that; it was not the beginning of his existence; the pre-existent Son was made that.

Then, if Son, the Father and the Son were in that relationship before the incarnation.

And, since we are speaking of the LORD who changes not, whose name is The Eternal, we need not suppose that divine relationships are more unstable or of less duration than the unchangeableness and eternity of his being.

In another place it is said, God gave his only begotten Son. Then he must have been that, to be given. Otherwise that was not the gift. But the Son was the gift.

Again 'God sent his only begotten Son into the world.' Then he must have been the only begotten Son before being sent into the world. Otherwise, it would not have been true to say that the Son was sent. On the contrary, if the relationship commenced from the incarnation, as some erroneously teach, then he would have had to be sent in order to become the Son.

But it does not say that he came to be the Son. It says 'God sent his only begotten Son.' Then he was the Son before the sending.

In the parable of the vineyard, God sent many messengers, each of whom was more or less ill-treated. This indicated the prophets and wise men whom God had sent since righteous Abel, since Israel was called out of Egypt, and up until the sending of the prophet Zacharias. But it all did no good: every one was maltreated.

However, 'having yet one Son' — he had one Son, held in reserve over all that time — he sent him last of all.

Not he sent one to be the Son. No, having sent all those prophets to no profit, and still having his only Son with him, he sent the Son last of all. Not to be the Son. He was the Son, and since Abel, through Israel, until Zacharias, God had him yet.

Then he sent him in the fulness of time. So he existed from the beginning and therefore in the form of God, and if so in the relationship of Son. It was just a question of when he should be sent. Not of what his relationship should be upon the sending.

Once more. The apostle says, God sent his own Son in the likeness of sinful flesh. That was the likeness after the sending: it was certainly not the likeness before the sending.

27

He was Son before being sent: when he was sent, he appeared in that likeness. Before being sent the self-existent person of the Son was solely in the likeness of God, and, with the Father and the Holy Ghost, subsisted in one divine essence from everlasting, three persons in one, spiritually indivisible: for God is a spirit.

Yet the revelation made known by the coming of the Son was not in the likeness of the glory which he had with the Father before the world was. Rather, it was in the likeness of sinful flesh veiling that glory. Nevertheless the revelation thus made known was of three persons in one, Father, Son, and Holy Ghost, of whom we can say in truth, From everlasting to everlasting thou art God.

Moreover, in the midst of the Old Testament, long, long before the coming of the Son and giving of the Holy Ghost, when God was utterly hidden behind the unrent veil and the Name spoken through the veil was Jehovah, then once and again, God — who is a spirit — spoke of what was in his eternal being and relations.

Of this the Hebrew writer quotes: 'Unto the Son he saith, Thy throne, O God, is for ever and ever.' Therefore, so is his eternal sonship.

Thus it was also, as looking forward through long ages to the incarnation and resurrection, that the Father said so many centuries before: 'Thou *art* my Son.'

And it must be so. Otherwise how could he be called — and he is called — 'The Son of the living God'? For this plainly declares that the nature of the life of God, 'the living God', is the duration of the relationship Son. 'The *Son* of the living God.'

But the nature of the life of God is everlasting life. Then the duration of the relationship Son is eternal sonship.

Moreover, given that eternal things cannot change — otherwise they would not be eternal — observe that in I John 1:2 the Word of life, that is, the Son of God, is described as 'that eternal life'. But if so, eternally Son.

And if any choose to quibble, they are silenced immediately by the continuation of the verse: 'That eternal life, which was with the Father.' Now, for how long was he with the Father? Obviously, eternally long. As long as eternal life. That is, as long as eternity. But in what relationship? 'With the Father.' There follows of necessity, eternal sonship.

By clearly asserting the eternity of the Father *as Father*, then of course in order to be valid this expression equally demands the everlasting relationship, Son.

Besides, as concerning the time when David called Christ 'Lord' — when Psalm 110 was written — Jesus says, If David called him Lord, 'Whose Son is he?' Matthew 22:42. That is, whose Son at the time at which David spoke, for then David called him 'Lord'.

Well of course, he must have been God's Son, for David certainly would not call one Lord who was merely his own son. That was exactly what Jesus was pointing out. David would never call Solomon Lord.

But the Son of God who was to be made of the seed of David according to the flesh some one thousand years later, yes, certainly, David would call him, 'Lord'. And he did.

From which it follows — 'Whose Son was he?' — that Christ's divine sonship is not in any way conditioned or derived from his humanity. He was Son a thousand years before!

But unbelieving reasoners will say, Impossible. But the fact remains, David did, it was written at the time, and so long afterwards the Lord Jesus himself interpreted the meaning we have given. Therefore it is the reasoning unbeliever that is impossible, not the eternity of Christ's sonship.

As to that, unbelieving reasoners stumble on the Rock of offence, and trip over the Stone of stumbling, as was foretold of them, and many since. What stone is this? Why, the stone of the eternal relationship of the Father and the Son.

Saith the Son, 'I and my Father are one.' But when do you suppose that oneness commenced, seeing that Christ is called 'the true God and eternal life'?

Like Melchizedek who depicted him, he is, Hebrews 7:3, 'Without father, without mother, without descent, having neither beginning of days, nor end of life; but made like unto the Son of God; abideth a priest continually.'

Now, if made like unto the Son of God — that is, made to appear so in a figure, by the deliberate wording of the narrative in Genesis 14, upon which Hebrews 7:3 comments — what does the writer to the Hebrews consider the distinguishing features of the Son of God?

The following: No descent. No beginning. That is, not to his sonship: his sonship has no descent and no beginning.

As to his human origin, 'Without father.' But as to his un-descended, never-beginning, continuously abiding, eternal sonship, Ever with the Father. Then the eternal Son.

That is the chief characteristic of his sonship, according to the writer unto the Hebrews.

Hence the Son says, 'Father, glorify thou me with thine own self with the glory which I had with thee before the world was.'

And what glory was that? Why obviously, since it is 'thine own self' in the name of 'Father' whom he addresses, the glory of the Father. But this same glory Jesus shared with him 'before the world was.' When was that? Before time began. That is, eternity. And what glory was it in eternity? The glory of the Father.

Now if Jesus shared the glory of the Father in eternity before the world was, he must have done so as Son of the Father. Then, eternal Son.

Beyond human and angelic understanding, this is not, cannot, and may not be explained. Nevertheless it is commanded to the obedience of faith to be believed, because it is the truth revealed by the Father regarding his only begotten Son.

'Whosoever transgresseth, and abideth not in the doctrine of Christ, hath not God. He that abideth in the doctrine of Christ, he hath both the Father and the Son,' II John 9. Where the knowledge of God is synonymous with the knowledge of the Father and the Son. It is the knowledge of God. That is what God is revealed to be by the Spirit. It is the revelation of the Eternal. The true God and eternal life. Absolutely, it is the revelation of eternal relationships. That is the doctrine of Christ.

'If there come any unto you, and bring not this doctrine, receive him not into your house, neither bid him God speed,' II John 10.

So that when we read of him upon whom we are to believe for salvation, he whom the gospel declares to be 'THE SON OF GOD', we are to understand this to assert and embrace two things:

the first, HIS EVERLASTING DEITY;

and the last, HIS ETERNAL SONSHIP.

Now these two things combine in one person and relationship to present to faith this most essential gospel revelation. Here is the truth of the Son of God for all who aspire for divine assent to their belief. These things, they must believe.

This concludes the meaning of the first of these great statements about Jesus Christ made by the apostle Paul at the beginning of the gospel: That he was the Son of God.

●  ●  ●

I PASS NOW to the next proposition. The scripture reads, 'Which was made of the seed of David according to the flesh,' Romans 1:3.

# II
# THAT HE WAS 'MADE'
# ACCORDING TO THE FLESH

One cannot but pause at such an expression. God's Son, Jesus Christ our Lord, made of the seed of David according to the flesh. Amazing.

Consider that here is no speculative theology; no obscure treatise irrelevant to common men; no tortuous philosophical reasoning without relevance to actual life. To the contrary, here is the sole divinely validated truth of the gospel. In its very essence.

It is God's revelation of God's gospel, concerning God's Son, given by God's apostle, that God's salvation might be expressed aright. It is the essence of the gospel. Only this has authority; but it has absolute authority, to command and assure the faith of every believer.

And yet for all that, such objective truth expounding

the person of Christ is so rarely heard. It is considered superfluous to the modern gospel. It is nothing to do with evangelism today. Something the church should take care of, not the ordinary person. Yet according to the holy apostles — the only true authority — it is what the individual must believe to be saved.

Observe therefore that truth presented to faith concerning the person of the Son of God and with his being made of the seed of David according to the flesh — basic gospel truth, according to Paul — is so different from the light and worldly, the warm and personalised, the good newsy, friendly neighbourhood 'Jesus' of modern christianity.

There is no resemblance. This is not an exaggeration; not a sweeping statement. Listen, look, see and compare: modern ministry and current evangelical trends bear no resemblance to the apostolic gospel. Nor to the apostolic method.

Indeed the average congregation has become so accustomed to this bland diet that it is questionable whether for them — if they should hear it — the apostolic gospel would not be uninteresting to the point of utter — though offended — boredom.

Nevertheless, it is this apostolic gospel with its apostolic doctrine, and its apostolic method, that is the sole means of salvation from faith to faith. Of deliverance from this world and justification for the world to come.

The gospel of our salvation insists that the Son of God was made of the seed of David according to the flesh. But why? Faith, true faith feels that she must understand why. And will understand why as, believing, with eagerness and meekness she absorbs the doctrine with all her heart and mind.

We have learned that if the Son of God was so made, then he was pre-existent. If pre-existent as Son of God then divine. If divine then in the name and relationship of Son with the Father.

We have seen that this mystery is at the very heart of the gospel. It is the mystery of the gospel: Father, Son, and Holy Ghost, one God yet three persons, three persons yet one God.

This is what the coming of the Son made known: not intellectually, not for students to consider. Experimentally, for the saints, indwelt, to worship. How important his coming, then. And how important the He who came. If so, then the manner of his coming must be pre-eminent truth for faith to apprehend. Hence saith the Spirit of his coming 'made of the seed of David according to the flesh.'

Now then, the gospel opens with the coming forth of God's Son. He came in the fulness of time, and, coming, was 'made' or 'became of' the seed of David. How did this affect him? And how did it not?

Be assured:

- This did not entail the slightest alteration to his divine nature: it was the addition to it of his human nature.

- This was not to divest himself of his divinity: it was to clothe it with his humanity.

35

□ This was not to change his divine person or relationship in deity: it was to become incarnate in full possession of his unaltered and unalterable divine relationships and eternal Godhead.

Nevertheless, as found in fashion as a man, among men, to do the work he had come to accomplish, of necessity the Son of God laid aside the visible radiance of his divine glory. He divested himself of the unapproachable light that no man hath seen nor can see. He veiled the unbearable blaze before which even the seraphs must perforce cover their faces.

Of necessity, I say, he put by him the awe-inspiring signs that manifested the presence of his glorious Deity. He relinquished the appearance of that dreadful omnipotence that characterised the visitations of the Most High. He hid behind him the overwhelming might by which he made the worlds and then upheld all things by the word of his power.

He showed no sign of the terribleness of his majesty by which he shall dissolve the elements, melt the essence of matter with fervent heat, roll up the heavens as a scroll, fold the universe as a vesture, and burn away the earth with heat unimaginable.

These things would have been seen had he not hid them, but kindly, he laid aside every sign of them. He obscured every external appearance, every outward manifestation of who he was when

'being in the form of God,
he thought it not robbery to be equal with God:

'But made himself of no reputation,
and took upon him the form of a servant,
and was made in the likeness of men:
'Being found in fashion as a man.'

But his intrinsic deity, that itself was unaltered. Only the outshining and manifestation of it was prevented by his own voluntary humiliation. So that what he was made, veiled the He who was made it. But that is all it was: a veil. 'The veil, that is to say, his flesh,' says the writer to the Hebrews.

And that is the emphasis here. 'Which was made of the seed of David according to the flesh.' How thin the veil!

How thin the veil. 'He was in the world, and the world was made by him.' 'Yet the world knew him not'? Knew him not, and yet the veil so thin? How refined, how translucent, the veil of flesh that hid him. Then what made him so obscure to men?

'He came unto his own, and his own received him not.' Yet the flesh he was made was foretold — of the seed of David — and were it not, how could it hide Jehovah from the Jews? But it did. 'For had they known, they would not have crucified the Lord of glory.' Made of the seed of David. But they would not even own the seed, much less the Maker.

Because the deity of the Son is being stressed in Romans 1:3, his humanity is not. It is not the human nature of the Lord Jesus that is in mind: only the actual body considered in and of itself. And even then, hardly that. For his body is referred to only as 'seed' and 'flesh'. Not actually 'body'.

37

Nothing here about his human life, soul, spirit, mentality, feelings, passions, volition, imagination, reason, will, affections, consciousness.

Nothing of his human nature: that for which the body is the vehicle of expression. How fully that is spoken of and illustrated elsewhere! But it certainly is not the emphasis here. It is not mentioned here. I repeat, not even the word 'body' occurs here.

Neither do we hear in this place of the virgin being with child nor of the virgin birth. Jesus' birth, infancy, development: these things are not mentioned, that is not the stress here, though it is elsewhere.

Romans 1:3-4, the very substance, the heart, the essential summary of the gospel, commences with the person of Christ as made known in order by the Holy Ghost.

Through God's commandment the holy apostle, infallibly declaring the gospel of God, once and for ever directs the faith of all believers, recording the word of God in holy scripture. And what is the first and pre-eminent truth to which the Lord's apostles direct our belief?

This: that the gospel of God emphasises the pre-existent and eternal Son of God. That *he* was the one who was manifest in the flesh; not so much the flesh in which he was manifested; rather, the He who was manifested in it.

First we are to know who was made of the seed of David according to the flesh. This is what one's faith must lay hold upon in the gospel.

It is God's gospel. God wrought it. It is all of God. And all concerning God's Son.

Who is this person? What has he done? What has been done to him? This is what the gospel declares. Everything is divine. And everything, but everything, concerns Christ in person. There is no other doctrine.

The gospel first stresses just who it was that 'came according to the flesh.' The accent is not yet upon that humanity which the Son of God took to himself when he became incarnate. First it is upon the Son himself. Before he did anything, he was: the eternal Son. And when he had done everything, he remained, unchanged, the same: the everlasting Son of God.

That is what must be grasped first of all: Who it is that was made flesh.

All that is true of his humanity — no doubt implied here — is in fact explicitly and fully dealt with elsewhere. What is stressed here in the beginning of the gospel is the nature of the person that became incarnate: I repeat, just who it was that was hidden by the veil of flesh.

In Romans 1:3 strictly it is the incarnation that is the primary emphasis. Incarnation proper speaks of the body alone. If so, then the stress is upon the one whose body this was. It emphasises the deity and eternity of the Son of God who in taking that veil of flesh was himself brought so near to men. 'For the Life was manifested, and we have seen it ... which was with the Father, and was manifested unto us.'

That is it: not the humanity here. Not the human nature

first. But first that which was first. The eternity of the Son of God. Only now, seen in the flesh. God manifest in the flesh. 'In-carnate' meaning 'in-fleshed'. The 'seed', the 'flesh', accentuates the deity indwelling that flesh, not the flesh itself. The great emphasis is upon GOD. It is he. Just as it is his gospel entirely wrought by him.

On the other hand, because we receive this primary emphasis, as instructed by the apostle who teaches us the gospel, we do not therefore lose sight of what is taught elsewhere. We will not be caught off balance, because we receive what is taught in all the gospel as well as in this the beginning of it.

Therefore we shall be perfectly balanced. The reason is this: placing the emphasis in its correct apostolic order and precedence, as we have done, the weight of the truth will be properly and evenly distributed in our doctrine.

Having reached this point, we make the following observations:

When the Son of God was made of the seed of David according to the flesh, he did not:

□ Change into a man.

□ Indwell a man.

□ Or merely — despite the emphasis of Romans 1:3 — *merely* become incarnate.

Then what did he do?

He was 'made' according to the flesh.

He was 'made' says the translation. In the original Greek the word is γενομένου, from γίνομαι, *ginomai, to come into being.* This one Greek word occurs some six hundred and twenty times in the New Testament. Nevertheless the translators have managed to find no less than forty different English words into which to split the occurrences.

Surely the essence of translation is to find a single word in one's native tongue — not so difficult — answering to that one word in the original, and then stick to it. In this case our clerical scholars have settled for forty.

However, forty native English words answering to one single original Greek word is not the whole story of this completely typical ineptitude.

Out of these forty English alternatives arbitrarily selected by the committee of ecclesiastics: twenty-three times they have used single English words — to translate *ginomai* — once and once only.

Over and above all this they have used yet a further ten entirely different English words to translate *ginomai* for no more than two or three occasions per word.

Notwithstanding, if multiple, these are the minor lacerations. The major renderings into which the learned butchers from the old Anglican abattoir have hacked the poor corpse of *ginomai* are as follows:

Be . . . . . . . . . . . . . . . 249 times.
Come . . . . . . . . . . . . . . 53 times.
Arise . . . . . . . . . . . . . 16 times.
Be made . . . . . . . . . . . . 69 times.

Be done . . . . . . . . . . . . 62 times.
Come to pass . . . . . . . . 82 times.
Become . . . . . . . . . . . . 42 times.

From the sum of which possibly it might be deduced that the word *ginomai* means *to come into being*. It might, but then this has been wondrously disguised by a bewildering and totally unnecessary multiplicity.

However in fact the word means, *to be, come, be-come*. Surely they could have found us a word for this? Or at least reduced it to two or three, not multiply it by forty! Especially when many of the forty are not even attempting to translate: they are barefaced interpretations.

But the sole and exclusive work of the translator is to give the people the word of God by translating the selfsame words of God into their own native tongue. No more. No less.

This has not happened with *ginomai* in Romans 1:3. It is not 'was made'. That is interpretive. It is not what *ginomai* means. The text should translate *ginomai* strictly and accurately. Then we should have something like:

'Who *came* of the seed of David according to
the flesh.'

— *as The Englishman's
Greek New Testament.*

Others have it:

*'come* of the seed of David ...'

Or:

'Who *is come* of the seed of David ...'

Whatever, let them give us *ginomai;* not use their translation opportunities as an occasion *to write into the word of God their opinionative interpretation* of the passage.

However, to continue with Romans. That is, now that we have understood what words the Holy Ghost himself useth, conveying the same to us through the disciplined fidelity of the holy apostle.

Hence what is being taught us is this: The Son of God who ever was, at a certain point in time came of the seed of David according to the flesh. That is, came into the world; came in the flesh.

Thus it is a question of how he came.

As to the importance of this, judge ye:

'Every spirit that confesseth that Jesus Christ
is come in the flesh is of God;
'And every spirit that confesseth not that
Jesus Christ is come in the flesh is not of
God: and this is that spirit of antichrist,'

*I John 4:2,3.*

But this confession is not blind: it must be understood.

Now then, as to that flesh in which he came, this sets before us the work of Almighty God, Father, Son and Holy Ghost. The coming required the divine creation from

Mary's substance and life of a real body, true human
nature, and essential human life. This entailed:

1. The authority of the Father.
2. The operation of the Spirit.
3. The incarnation and assumption of the Son.

And it involved the divine persons in their divine
activities in relation to Mary, of the house of David, a virgin
of Nazareth, in Galilee, espoused to one Joseph of the
house of David, of that same city.

Now these things are clearly taught in Matthew 1:1-25
and in Luke 1:30-35. *

But they are not taught, much less emphasised, in
Romans 1:3. There, we read only of the fact of incarnation,
not of how it took place nor of the human nature involved:
simply of the bare fact that the Son of God 'is come of the
seed of David according to the flesh.'

In the passage in Romans we read nothing of Mary,
her conception, or of the virgin birth. Neither Jesus'
genealogy †, nor his human nature nor perfect humanity.
Implied, certainly. But implied precisely because actually
taught elsewhere as concerning the birth of Jesus Christ.

Because the truth is one, everything from the apostolic
revelation of the gospel must be included — by implication
— at any given point in the doctrine of Christ. But if so,
truth taught in its own place and context must first be

---

* See 'The Birth of Jesus Christ'. The Publishing Trust, price 45p.
† See 'The Messiah', pages 6-22. The Publishing Trust, price £1.20.

fully weighed and its omissions, inclusions and emphases carefully noted before being carried over to other passages on the same subject. So that when the whole of the revelation from every place is drawn together under one head, nothing is missing from each distinct part.

This means that every relevant passage — such as Romans 1:3 — first must be evaluated as if nothing were taught elsewhere. Only then can its teaching contribute in full measure to the whole doctrine relating to the birth of Jesus Christ, gathered from every place wherever the subject is taught.

Hence we are to notice what is stated in Romans; also what is not stated; then what is the full force of that statement. Finally we are to include by implication what is taught elsewhere as it bears upon the incarnation.

It is with this in mind — the inclusion of what has been taught elsewhere as it bears upon the incarnation — that I pause to hear and answer certain questions that arise as regards the coming of the Son of God 'of the seed of David according to the flesh.'

*Question 1. Was this seed the seed of a man?*

No. Of a woman, singularly. If so, the seed of a virgin. In fact, of the virgin Mary, of the ancestry, house and lineage of David. Therefore it was 'of the seed of David according to the flesh.'

*Question 2. Was this woman immaculate?*

Certainly not. There is none righteous, no, not one. Not

45

one born of man and woman. Since Adam, death passed to all men, for that all have sinned. It is by one man's offence that death reigns. One man's disobedience brought the whole race under inbred sin.

Mary required an offering of two sacrificial birds 'According to that which is said in the law of the Lord,' Luke 2:24.

From this it is evident that strict justice found indwelling sin in Mary, as with all mankind in the fall. And with this verdict Mary herself had no quarrel: she made the offering.

Otherwise how could justice demand sacrifice 'according to the *law* of the Lord'? It was a matter of law. Sacrifice would have been superfluous — and hence lawless — had Mary been immaculate.

Sacrifice was not a mere *custom:* it was the absolute demand of God's holiness. That is what the law of the Lord found. Law is not arbitrary. The fact of sacrifice is conclusive evidence that inbred sin had been discovered and required atonement before worship could be resumed.

That is, sin was discovered in Mary.

But not in her seed. When Mary conceived of the Holy Ghost, that seed — though truly created from her body and life — nevertheless was immaculate. Called 'that holy thing', no sin had tainted it, none had passed to it, it was spotless, without sin.

But Mary herself was not. Inbred sin from the fall was as common to her as to all men. Like death its consequence — sin *passed* to all men.

## Question 3. Was this seed immaculate?

Absolutely. It was absolutely impeccable. It was the holy seed, the seed of the woman, the seed of promise, the promised seed of Abraham and the seed of David. It was without spot or blemish. Completely pure.

This holy seed to be born of Mary had been so divinely overshadowed and inwrought that there never was any contact with the inbred sin in life, nature and substance common to all mankind. How could there be? It was, by definition 'that holy thing', Luke 1:35.

Holy. So holy as to be suited, actually suited, for the incarnation and assumption of the Son of God from heaven. 'Therefore also that holy thing which shall be born of thee shall be called the Son of God.'

This 'body prepared' for the coming of the Son was without sin; that is, without that inbred corruption or sin passed upon all men since the fall of Adam. This unique promised seed was truly man but 'sin apart'. That is, 'apart' as a result of the creative operation of the Holy Ghost in the very formation of the seed.

So that upon the instant of divine creation in the womb of the virgin, even before that point, from the very first moment of the existence of any element involved, absolute purity from any taint of the fall was assured.

Thus the perfection of conception took place. Because the seed of the woman was immaculate. It was suited for the coming of him who 'abhorred not the virgin's womb,' the Son of God, 'come of the seed of David according to the flesh.'

*Question 4. Was this seed a body only?*

No, it was more than a body that was created from the seed of the woman by 'the Holy Ghost coming upon Mary, and the power of the Highest overshadowing her.'

A body *was* created: 'Wherefore when he cometh into the world' — that is, when the Son of God cometh into the world — 'he saith, Sacrifice and offering thou wouldest not, but a body hast thou prepared me.' A body was created. But more than a body only.

'The seed of the woman' must be more than a body only. That seed is not only of Mary's substance: it must be alive, and if so, alive with *her* life. She was told, *Thou* shalt conceive. She herself. It is her seed, and her life quickened that seed.

This is that which was holy from the inception of its very elements. This is that from which the Holy Ghost, coming upon Mary, created within her womb — 'Thou shalt conceive in thy womb' — the body prepared for the coming of the Son of God. Flesh of Mary's flesh, bone of her bone, life of her life.

Even more than that. In that chosen seed were all the qualities of human nature also. It was said to Mary, 'Thou shalt bear a *child.*' Mary is called 'his mother Mary'.

Real human character and spirit are seen in the Lord Jesus. All the faculties and attributes of the soul are evident in him. Then that seed possessed true humanity: real human nature.

Otherwise, how could he weep, tire, thirst, pray, ponder,

sigh, sleep, hunger, yearn, feel, think, perceive, submit, determine, sorrow, joy, praise and worship?

But he did. As no man had done before him. He was the Son of man. He is the man Christ Jesus. He is not ashamed to call us brethren.

Then why do some places speak only of his body? For example, Romans 1:3? That speaks only of his body: 'Of the seed of David according to the flesh.' And Hebrews 10:5, 'A body hast thou prepared me.' Only the body is referred to there. And so it is with several other passages. But why?

Because that is what they wish to point out. Or rather, by omitting reference to his entire humanity and pointing only to the flesh, they thereby emphasise the deity and divine nature of the one whose body it is. By muting the fulness of his humanity, they thereby articulate the mystery of his deity.

This places the accent upon the eternal, the divine, the everlasting Son of God. He is the one incarnate within this body. He is the one made of the seed of David according to the flesh.

It is the Son of God so thinly veiled. That is the stress of our passage in Romans. But it is not the only stress. Nor the stress everywhere.

Each place must be fully weighed, to get the good of all the revelation. Some speak of his body only, the flesh in which the Son of God came. Others, his humanity, the man that he is, how human he was. 'Behold the man,' they say. In any given place, it is a question of emphasis.

*Question 5. Was this seed a human person?*

No. Absolutely not. It was manhood created for a divine person, that is, the Son of God. It is the body and humanity of the divine person of the Son.

The created seed possessed all the properties of human nature, but this human nature was exclusively that of the Son. He was the person whose it was. It was his true humanity. There was not and there could not be, any question whatsoever of a human person. Absolutely not.

What we see revealed is *a divine person with a human nature.*

Therefore the humanity of the Son of God appears at once as unique. It is a manhood outside of all precedent, past all measure, and beyond any comparison. The human nature of the divine person of the Son of God.

There exists here a distinction which it is essential for professing believers to perceive and distinguish in the knowledge of our Lord and Saviour Jesus Christ.

Failure to do so has led many from ignorance to darkness, from darkness to error, and from error to unbelief. Such make void in their minds the truth that 'Jesus Christ is come in the flesh.'

The seed of the woman, this seed of David, was not a human person. His humanity was true human nature — sin apart — but not a human person. It was the unique created humanity of the person of the Son of God. But it, itself, could not be a person. How could it?

It could not, for three reasons. Consider those reasons:

### The first reason

Lies in the realisation of what, in the normal sense, brings a person into being. The existence of a human being, a true human personality, takes place upon conception. It does not, and it cannot, occur through the mere existence of the male seed. That seed is actually part of the male person to whom it pertains.

Neither does it, nor can it, occur by the mere existence of the female seed. That seed also is no more than a distinct part of the female person to whom it belongs.

Although real life and distinct substance exist in each of the separate seeds, that life and substance has no identity in itself. It is not more than a part of the actual life and substance of that man or woman respectively whose person gives it identity. That is what it is and all that it is: despite its potential, it is in fact the seed of the person to whom it belongs.

For a human being, a person, to come into existence, there must be a fusion of the two seeds — male and female — into one, so creating an entirely new entity. Fusion must take place, union, life to life and substance to substance, to form a new distinct life and unique personal substance. That of the person who has thus come into being.

The two seeds, male to female, must become one within the woman before a human being — a person — comes into existence. It is not until the real and effective union into one of the male seed and the female that a new personality is conceived into human being.

But, with Mary's seed: that never happened.

The seed of David according to the flesh was never — as to human origin — anything other than the singular seed of the woman.

Then however amazing, however divine, whatever wonderful creation took place: it was not and could not be the bringing into existence of an actual human person, a distinct human being.

For this simple reason: there was no male seed. It was the seed of the woman alone. And this the holy scripture is most careful to safeguard.

And no wonder. For without this care, the person of Jesus Christ, 'come in the flesh', would never rightly be understood. And if not rightly understood, then not properly believed upon. And if not properly believed upon, then we would be yet in our sins and our faith found vain.

*The second reason.*

Though the seed is called 'the seed of David', obviously, since over one thousand years separated David himself from the birth of Jesus Christ, the meaning is general. We are to understand: 'of the house and lineage of David.'

In particular, it was a daughter of that house, Mary, who bare the seed. It was the seed of the virgin singularly.

This seed consisted of two parts: life of Mary's life, and substance of her substance.

Therefore the creative work of the Holy Ghost consisted of two parts.

First, to create from the life of Mary a perfection of humanity in which no inherent concupiscence and no intrinsic iniquity existed. Though that was in Mary's life, it was not in the human nature created from it by the Holy Ghost.

Second, to create from the substance of Mary a perfect body in which no taint or stain of inbred sin ever appeared or even had the remotest contact. Though that was in Mary's substance, it was not in the body created from it by the Holy Ghost.

Only thus could the seed be impeccable. But thus it was impeccable.

In this manner there was created — by as real a creative act of God as any in the creation — a manhood perfect and void of all natural corruption and bias in human life and substance from the fall.

Albeit this creative work was wrought in so minute a seed, nevertheless the nature of the work, its constant overshadowing and divine protection, assured that some nine months after the event 'that holy thing which shall be born of thee shall be called the Son of God.'

But now consider that moment of creation itself, nine months prior to the birth of Jesus Christ. What happened?

At that very moment came to pass the saying:

'The Holy Ghost shall come upon thee.'

And immediately the work was done, that is, the twofold creative work of the Holy Ghost described above.

However, that was not all that took place at that self-same moment.

Simultaneously with this creative work of the Holy Ghost, the incarnation — conception — of the Son took place.

Carefully consider this distinction in the following passages:

> 'That which is conceived in her
> is of the Holy Ghost.'

> 'Thou shalt conceive in thy womb,
> and bring forth a son.'

> 'Behold, a virgin shall be with child,
> and shall bring forth a son,
> and they shall call his name Emmanuel.'

Instantaneous with the work of the Spirit, conception took place through the work of the Son. But conception of a nature that had never occurred before. Conception so unique, so spiritual, so divine, that only revelation can convey what took place.

No parallel exists nor can exist from the beginning of the world to the end of it, from the commencement of time till time shall be no more.

Conception, yes. But of so stupendous a character that only divine condescension could warrant the use of that word. For this conception has nothing in common with that proper to the bringing into being of a human person.

There, the male seed penetrates the female and both are fused into one. Here,

1. There was no male seed.

2. Nothing physical or material — extraneous to Mary — was introduced in any way or at any time whatsoever.

3. There existed solely the female seed.

4. What took place was entirely spiritual, and wholly divine.

5. What the Holy Ghost created was entirely from the seed of the woman.

6. That in which the Son of God simultaneously became incarnate was precisely what the Holy Ghost had instantaneously created, without the introduction of any physical or material agency.

7. The incarnation was thus an entirely spiritual act on the part of the Son of God in respect of the 'body prepared' by the Holy Ghost under the overshadowing of the Most High.

   Then the conception was unique, in that it was divine. In that it was not in the remotest way physical. In that it was in respect of what the Holy Ghost created from the seed of the woman. In that it was an entirely spiritual act of incarnation and assumption by the Son of God.

Whence it follows of necessity that the seed of the woman prepared by the Holy Ghost and received by the Son of God was true human nature but not a human person.

It follows because the creative work of the Spirit was from the seed of the woman singularly.

And it follows because 'conception' here means that the Son assumed the human nature prepared for him as his own manhood in incarnation. It was specifically the manhood of the person of the Son of God. *He* was the person whose *it* was, and to whom it pertained.

The understanding of 'conception' — in this unique instance of the word — clearly reveals this truth.

The instant in which the Holy Ghost created the impeccable 'seed of David' from Mary's life and flesh, simultaneously 'conception' took place.

This peerless use of 'conception' teaches that the person of the Son of God took that humanity which the Holy Ghost had prepared. The Son united that life with his own; assumed that human nature into union with his divine nature; and instantly became incarnate within that seed.

Given that human nature is the distinctive medium or expression of that human being to whom it belongs, and from whom it is absolutely inseparable, then consider the truth of Christ's manhood.

It is unique beyond all understanding, wonderful. It passes knowledge, amazing. It is revelation beyond all reason, commanding faith alone. Divine.

Here is human life. A true human soul. A real body. Entire humanity; human nature to the fullest. Yet unlike any other. First in that it is without sin. But above all in that it was created uniquely from the seed of the woman by the Holy Spirit of God.

Unlike any other! For all other human nature is the distinctive possession of the human person to whom it is united and from whom it is inseparable. Not this! This unique human nature is the distinctive possession of the divine person who united it to himself and who has made it inseparably his by the incarnation.

The eternal Son of God is the person. The created seed of David is his humanity.

### The third reason

— proving the negative to Question 5, Was this seed a human person? — follows from the truth of the unity of Christ's person.

Hold clear the undeniable truth that Christ was one. Then immediately we are committed irrevocably to the belief that his humanity must be human nature and cannot be human person.

If anyone denies this, or impatiently brushes aside such a distinction between human nature and person as pointless and unnecessary, let them consider what they are saying.

They are saying one of two things. Either that Christ was not one person at all, or that it does not matter what he was.

But whosoever denies him, he will deny. And whosoever cares nothing about him, he will care nothing about. And anyone saying it does not matter who he is, or what he was, in turn will find the Judge caring nothing about who that person is, or what he was. Since he preferred to know nothing about Christ, in that day he will discover that Christ says to him, 'I never knew you.'

Anyone presuming that the seed of the woman was a human being, denies the unity of Christ's person. Worse. By his folly he is inevitably trapped into the position of asserting that Christ must have been two persons, one divine and now also one human. This raises the ancient error of duality of person.

But the truth is, Christ is one person! Profound, peerless, and incomparable.

Furthermore, we are called and required to believe and receive the truth about his unique being. One person; having within that person, without confusion, a duality of natures: one divine and one human, one eternal and one created.

From everlasting the Son of God was a divine person, possessed of the divine nature.

In time the Holy Ghost created from the seed of the woman what was and must be a human nature. It was not and could not be a human person.

That human nature the Son of God united with his divine nature in the integrity of his one person. Thus within that one person we see two natures in duality without confusion. A singularity of person but a duality of nature.

The possession — the very existence — of human nature without human person is unique to the Son of God. As such his manhood stands apart completely.

Human nature, body, soul, and life, is considered as that belonging to the person whose it is for human self-expression. And in the case of every human being born of man and woman that is true. Human nature is the vehicle of expression for the person, for the self-conscious identity, for the ego itself, the being.

In the unique case of the humanity of the Son of God that person or being was not human but divine. Not a human being but a divine person.

The eternal being, the identity, the 'I AM' of the Son of God is from everlasting to everlasting. And so is his divine nature.

But not his human nature. The person of the Son took that human nature as the vehicle of his human expression.

What a staggering, what a wonderful thing this is! Oh, stupendous.

In the unique case of the Son of God, his humanity neither belonged to nor existed for a human being. It was created for the human expression of the divine being of the Son of God.

Otherwise the Son of God would merely have indwelt a man. But he did not. He became incarnate in his own body. He took into union his own human nature. And he did so for evermore. Amen.

Now then:

▢ As to the Body.  The Son of God became incarnate.

▢ As to the Soul.  He took that whole mentality, sensibility, volition — withal the entire human nature — and united it in one but without confusion, with his divine nature.

▢ As to the Life.  This he received into union — again without confusion — with his own eternal divine life.

Regarding his eternal person, possessed of his everlasting nature, his name is I AM. And as his name so is his divine nature. As it was, is now, and ever shall be, unchanged and unchanging.

But at the point of time referred to in 'made of the seed of David according to the flesh,' he, the eternal Son, became incarnate in that flesh. In so doing he united that human nature, new created, with his own uncreated and everlasting divine nature.

Thus he possessed both human and divine natures in one person.

Nature being considered as that vehicle or medium suited for the self-expression of the person to whom it belongs, what we can say of the Son is this: The divine nature of the eternal Son ever was that through which he expressed his divine being. But now there was created for that divine person another nature, a human nature, a vehicle for his human expression:

- ☐ This was his body. There was no question of its ever being any other. He became incarnate within his own body in perpetuity.

- ☐ This was his humanity. There was no possibility that he indwelt the humanity of another as a temporary manifestation. He assumed his own unique humanity for evermore.

- ☐ This was his life. There was no suggestion of his possessing transient human life afterwards to be discarded. He took true human life into union with the divine, united to himself immortally.

That is, entire human nature for this eternal divine person for evermore taken into union with himself.

Thus I conclude the final reason to the last question regarding what is implied from elsewhere in connection with the statement of Romans 1:3, that the Son of God came 'of the seed of David according to the flesh.'


To close this part of the doctrine I add five aphorisms by which the truth may be clarified.

*The first.*

In that the Son of God became of the seed of David according to the flesh, by so much he added to himself, that is to his divine person and divine nature.

### The second.

But how much did he add? He added human nature, only certainly not and under no circumstances human person or human personality. He added human nature — *the vehicle or means of expression of a person* — I say, he added human nature to his divine person or personality.

### The third.

From eternity unchanged, ever expressed through his divine nature, now his person is also expressed through his created human nature, which he has taken into perpetual union with himself.

### The fourth.

He is not changed. His divine nature is unaltered. He has not changed into manhood in any way. Unchanged from eternity he has now *added* to himself that manhood through which also he will now and for ever express his divine person.

### The fifth.

So that as he was, thus he is and ever shall be, unchanged and unchanging in person and nature. But the *expression* of that person, now that he has taken to himself real manhood, is enhanced in true humanity also. He himself is now seen in an entirely new way. That of the Son

'come of the seed of David according to the flesh.'

It is this expression in manhood, both as to his person and work, that is the subject of the gospel. The gospel declares the expression.

'For the life was manifested, and we have seen it, and bear witness, and show unto you that eternal life, which was with the Father, and was manifested unto us.'

★

But why the emphasis on David?

Why 'come of the seed of *David* according to the flesh'?

Why not 'seed of the woman'; or 'of Mary'; or why not simply 'flesh' or 'man'?

Why reach back over one thousand years and more, to a man not a woman, and insist 'seed of David according to the flesh'? For the immediate fact was that the Son of God came of the seed of Mary according to the flesh.

But the doctrine in this place omits Mary, refers to her remote line of ancestry, goes back over one whole millennium, points not to a woman at all but a man, and a man deceased these one thousand years.

Neither Mary, nor her seed, nor womanhood, are mentioned at all. The reference is to that male figure, from so very long ago, who was her remote ancestor.

63

Nevertheless the Holy Ghost insists by the apostle, 'seed of *David* according to the flesh,' saying in another place, II Timothy 2:8,

> 'Remember that Jesus Christ
> of the seed of David
> was raised from the dead
> according to my gospel.'

'Remember,' says the aged apostle, peering from the brink of the grave into the last times, through this present time, until the end of time, unto the very coming of the Lord:

'Remember!' he cries to us.

Memory is the faculty advised.

'Remember my gospel.' For without it, you shall not be saved, faith having no sure resting place, belief no foundation, trust no revelation on which to rest. Remember my gospel.

'For I am now ready to be offered,' saith Paul the aged. 'The time of my departure is at hand,' cries the great and faithful apostle to the Gentiles. 'I have finished my course.'

'But my father, my father' — we call down the ages of infidelity, of apostasy, of sacramentalism, of priestcraft, of spiritual wickedness in high places, of subtle errors untold, of the rents in the unity of the body, of the fragmentation of the one faith, of the brokenness of the testimony into sectarianism, of neglect of the gospel, of the abhorrence of doctrine, of the quenching of the Spirit, of the departure of the glory, of the coming of unbelief. Of liberalism,

modernism, of worldliness, of materialism, of prayerless-
ness, of presumption. Of apathy, coldness, deadness, of the
great falling away — 'My father, my father,' we cry, 'Hast
thou not a blessing for us, even for us also?'

Yes, my son, he saith, Yes, for thee also.

For what more can he say to bless us also than this?
'Remember my gospel.'

Remember what was in the beginning. And particularly,
Remember that Jesus Christ of the seed of David was raised
from the dead according to my gospel. My gospel. There
are others. More and more. But not one of them is his
gospel, remember.

Then how important this truth of Jesus Christ of the
seed of David. At such a time he urges it; when he himself
had so little time, and so few words, left to live and speak
on earth. 'Of the seed of David.' How important it must
be.

But does one ever hear it stressed? Or preached? Or even
mentioned? Then what have we come to? Well, the answer
is obvious: we have come to forget. Forgetfulness. We have
come to disregard the memory. Then let us inquire with
insistence! What does it mean, that it is so very important?

Now then, declares the Holy Ghost in the gospel of
God sent to us Gentiles, now then, the Son of God came
according to the flesh. But not any flesh. David's flesh.
That is essential to the doctrine of the gospel.

Yet today it is hardly if ever heard, much less understood. And were it heard, most that consider themselves

Christians — yes, and 'keen' Christians at that — would shrug it off as of no interest. Not meaningful. Not relevant to the modern outlook. Not tuned in to today's scene. Not even evangelistic.

Others, a small elitist clique, as they like to think, would shuffle off to their church history, their puritans, their reformers, their creeds and confessions, to see if they should make anything of it according to the traditions of their fathers. Like truffle-hogs nosing in the stale earth, these snuffle and sniff through their old leaves and dead tomes which they remember.

Any other memory, any memory back to the beginning, must find its place subject to this opinionative tradition which these book-keepers, librarians, have collected long since. Otherwise, it could not be meaningful.

Well, I tell you, it is meaningful to the Day of judgment. It is relevant to the great Day of the Lord. It is attuned to the sound of eternity. And nothing else is, but this gospel. This gospel, remember?

Relevant, because what you believe about Jesus Christ, his person and his work, will determine your immortal destiny.

Meaningful, because what will determine your present faith, attuning it to eternity, is the meek reception of this very same doctrine. Remember.

But what does it mean, Of the seed of *David* according to the flesh?

For faith may be shining-eyed, she may be adoring, but

she is no fool! She is well-informed, and will be well-informed. She knows whom she believes, and adores whom she knows, and well studies the sight, crying constantly to the Spirit and the word, What meaneth these things?

And she shall not be sent empty away.

• • •

Now therefore observe how the Son of God came according to the flesh: it was as the seed of David. This leads to the third great statement of the apostle in his summary of the gospel of God concerning his Son:

# III

# THAT HE WAS 'MADE'
# OF THE SEED OF DAVID

# The Seed of David

WHY David?

Partly because of David's own distinctive ancestry and genealogy. Also because of the ancient promises made to and embodied in him. And because of the breeding and potential of character inherent in David's seed to his successors.

A vast heritage, you see, a unique inheritance, lay in store for David's heir. And referring to the Son of God 'made' according to the flesh we are saying 'This is the heir.'

Therefore 'of David' implies much more than inheritance considered as an exterior possession. Far more inward and intrinsic to 'of David' is that which is latent for David's successors as a matter of breeding; a true son to David will reflect that breeding and character.

More also is seen in that David was a type or figure of his coming seed: to understand this particular, one must consider David himself according to the flesh.

Why David?

Not least because that which is seen in David is more reflective of Christ, his humanity, his office, than has been or could be shown by any other person. It is not just a question of ancestry: it is a question of resemblance. Here perhaps more deeply than anywhere else one can say of a truth, This is the heir.

Consider David, then. What stands out about him?

There is the record in holy scripture. It can be read by

all. But in chapter after chapter of historical sequences and details one must discover common denominators, one must extract the essential traits.

What was paramount in David? What was in the mind of God, what answered to his heart, what was his purpose in David?

Three things stand out:

FIRST, DAVID WAS A MAN.

NEXT, DAVID WAS AN HEIR.

LAST, DAVID WAS A KING.

And now let us see what is 'of David' by considering each salient feature in turn.

## ¶ FIRST, DAVID WAS A MAN.

But what kind of a man was he? Well, at once strangely childlike, trusting, open and direct, a man in whose spirit was no guile: yet withal of great depth of soul, profound and complex, eluding easy definition.

He was of noble outlook, he possessed great breadth of mind, originality of character, much largeness of heart, much force of passion.

He was a man above pettiness. Generous; of ample magnanimity. Kind, and ready to forgive.

A man who had been down to the great deeps. He had

known well, long, and often the sourness of that bile which rises when the last hope sinks. He had full drunk the gall of bitterness; he had tasted the taste of despair. He had bitten the dust of death.

David had been to the depths and drunk to the full. But he had come back. The LORD had brought him back. 'O magnify the LORD with me, and let us exalt his name together.'

He was a singular man. His loneliness had ached and yawned and its echo had mocked him unrequited. He was a man apart. Yet he yearned for company, he was naturally gregarious.

But 'I sat alone because of thy hand.' He was set apart. With hollow groans he looked for some to pity, for one to understand; but there was no man, no, not any. His cry was lost to the desert and his groan trailed away in the sky. He was shut up to God: as to man David suffered the pangs alone.

Yes, he was a man who had been to the depths. Who had been tried to the limits of human endurance. And been tried again and again and again. Yet his resolution could not be broken. 'My heart is fixed, O God, my heart is fixed.' Could not be broken.

So he was a man of pity, suffering did not leave him unmoved, he was tender with a solicitude like that of a woman. His bowels were quick to move with compassion.

Yet he was a man terrible in battle, fearful in vengeance. Once drawn the sword, woe unto David's enemies. He would not turn, he would not sheath, till all were utterly destroyed. There was no peace, no sueing for terms, to the wicked. David hated the wicked.

His enemies fell before his fierce anger. Cunning and unpredictable in strategy and tactics, time and again he outwitted, out-thought, outgeneralled, and utterly confounded his adversaries.

As to men, as to the armies of the alien, as to personal safety, even as to defeat, he had no fear. He did not know what it meant. But he feared the Lord greatly. He knew what that meant.

He was a man who defied worldly analysis. Just when they thought they knew him, or unwisely dismissed him — confounding his direct integrity for simple naïvety — then it was that new depths unfolded in his character, hitherto undisclosed.

The truth is, David was a man who was beyond the analysis of the worldly-wise. Criteria applied about which the ungodly were totally ignorant. Hence they could not know David.

Experiences divine and human had occurred to David that the lives of his critics had not touched even remotely. Then how could they understand David, whose experience had not compassed even so much as the utmost shallows of the deep pool of his humanity?

The understanding of David confounded the sages of this world. Precisely because he lived, moved, and had his being in a spiritual depth of inwardness beyond the realms of mundane existence.

He had an interior life of single-minded devotedness to God, a bright and instant awareness of God's ways, judgments, and counsels; a deep internal consciousness of God's immediate presence, that defied the knowledge of the knowing and worldly-prudent.

And to this day, the understanding of David defies the doctor and analyst, the priest and scribe, the thinker and philosopher of this present world even to begin to understand.

Well, Jesus Christ was of the seed of David according to the flesh.

David was a man whose overriding passion, whose consummate zeal, whose indefatigable purpose, whose profound spirituality, was to dwell in the secret place of the Most High, to abide under the shadow of the Almighty.

He had this secret awareness. He had the hearing ear, the seeing eye, the understanding heart; he had the taste of grace, the feel of experience, the touch of His hand, the savour of His anointing. David was a man, and a man to the utmost.

Divine movement brought and kept David in union and communion. He abode in the most immediate and intimate touch with the realm of the Spirit, the kingdom of heaven, the world to come, the atmosphere of eternity, and above all, with every breath and whisper from Father, Son and Holy Ghost.

Much he did not know: but more utterly he could not live.

David lived and died for God and God alone and he did both with every fibre of his intense, passionate and absolutely wholehearted being. He reached and stretched every nerve for the consummation of God's pleasure and his eternal purpose.

Now I say, this utterly confounded, out of all reach and sight, it lay beyond all understanding of worldly men. That is the thing about David.

And the Son of God came of the seed of David according to the flesh.

David was a man. A man who defied analysis. Yet still, certain traits appeared, certain features predominated, in the son of Jesse, and it would be wrong not to note them. But from whence shall they be gleaned?

He who would discern the depths of David's character must look further than the record of his life among men in the books of Samuel, Kings and Chronicles. Beyond that outward history — necessary as it is in its place — David's spirit is open, his soul laid bare, his heart exposed, his inmost being revealed, in another book altogether.

There, every secret of the interior is revealed. We see mirrored his sighs to God, his trembling before the Lord, his supplications and thanksgivings, his prayers and vows. Beyond the external history, I say, David himself is found in the Book of Psalms. It is there that the lover of David must look.

For what one must perceive about David — and therefore his seed — is that every one of his divine and inward traits, every deep and godly motive, every profound spiritual depth, had a source. This was not in himself. Not in family, friends or kin. Not in Israel, nor in this world.

That source lay in his intense, intensely personal, and utterly secret life before God. He lived to God, and God alone. And he did so inwardly. Hence it is written of this man:

> 'I have found David the son of Jesse,
> a man after mine own heart,
> which shall fulfil all my will.
>
> 'Of this man's seed
> hath God according to promise
> raised unto Israel a Saviour, Jesus.'

*Acts 13:22,23.*

That is the secret of David, and of his seed for ever. In the book of the psalms it is written. There it can be seen. There you shall read of it. In the volume of the book it is written of him. There it appears: David was a man.

This was the elect seed. This was the man whom God had chosen. David was the man anointed.

Consider briefly certain of the traits which characterised this man:

- **He was a man without fear.**

Save the fear of God. As a youth he slew a lion and a bear. As a stripling he stood alone when all the armies of Israel quailed and ran: David stood alone and slew the giant. No fear of man, nor praise of man, deflected David. He was without the fear of man. He was aloof from both the applause and the threats of the multitude.

- **He was a man of sorrows.**

How plain this is from the psalms. David was acquainted with grief. Heart-broken cries, pitiful anguish, groans of unendurable suffering, were wrung from the lips of David and recorded in the psalms. Here is language:

*(i)* Created by the inward spiritual exercises through which God put his poor servant.

*(ii)* Caused by the outward providences in which David was hounded, despised and rejected by his persecutors in Israel. And with which Israel concurred or to which the people were largely indifferent.

Deep were David's trials. Complete was his loneliness. 'Lord, remember David, and all his afflictions.' Come, see if there be any sorrow like unto his sorrow, that of David and his seed for ever.

- **He was a man of discipline.**

Discipline was a strong trait in David's character. He had certainly been disciplined by men. He surely disciplined himself. But above all this his life and lifetime were characterised by the discipline of God.

'Whom the Lord loveth he chasteneth, and scourgeth,'

was exemplified in the life of David; years of David's lifetime continued to show this truth.

Two things are predominant in consequence:

*(i)* He knew authority when he saw it.

For example, when King Saul was discovered asleep, David's mighty men said, 'God hath delivered thine enemy into thine hand.' But David replied, 'The Lord forbid that I should stretch forth mine hand against the Lord's anointed.'

Again, with Abigail, Nabal's wife. Though towering in his wrath against Nabal, though committed before his men to avenge insult, though raging to destroy Nabal and all that pertained to him: still, he stayed himself.

He despised not a woman's meek advice, he recognised instantly the authority inherent in Abigail's plea, and forthwith he turned his face, owning what was superior to his own counsel.

*(ii)* The other trait brought out in character by long chastening and discipline was obedience.

David was *instantly* obedient. And he never wavered, though that obedience brought him to barren places of suffering which he endured with unremitting deprivation for years. David's obedience was as constant as it was instantaneous.

No question of, What will they think? Nothing
of, I must see what the brethren say about it.
Not a word of, But what will happen if I do?
He did as he was told, and he did it immediately, because of the one who had told him to
do it. Fearless of men, disdaining applause,
unmoved by criticism: David did it, and did it
straightway.

- **He was a man of patience.**

'I waited patiently for the LORD.' Four times over he
asked 'How long, O Lord?' in the thirteenth psalm. But if
for ever, if till he dies, if till he sleep the sleep of death,
David will never give up waiting on the Lord: he will
neither turn to man, nor deliver himself.

'My soul waits for the Lord.' 'In the LORD put I my
trust.' This is David's language, and the language of his life
as well as of his lips. Patience and faith, faithfulness and
endurance, these things were characteristic of David. He
was a man of patience.

- **He was a man of vision.**

He saw things hidden from ordinary men. But like
chosen Joseph, who saw visions denied his brethren and
elders, after he told them what God had revealed to him,
they were filled with indignation.

The brethren did not appreciate God's particular choice
of his servant. Especially in order to inform them of
heavenly things they had neither seen nor known.

Nevertheless it was a fact, and God spoke to David and opened the eyes of the sweet psalmist of Israel. They must hear it from him or not hear it at all. David opened his mouth to utter sayings dark of old, he spoke in parables, he saw in the visions of the Almighty.

What visionary faith possessed this elect, this man of God's right hand. He ever had the ark of God on his heart, he brought up the ark. He knew what was in the mind of God, he saw what was his pleasure. He ever kept the house of God before his vision, Psalm 132.

What others despised, could not see, or thought impossible of realisation, David saw, believed, and achieved. He perceived in vision the house of God and its service, the assembly of God's people. This was his heavenly vision, his chiefest joy and pleasure, Psalm 122.

Ever the heavenly glory of the LORD was before David's opened eyes. Observe how he saw Christ in Psalm 45, his glory in Psalm 110, his renown in Psalm 2.

More, he saw in vision the body of Jesus, withal the body of Christ; he could distinguish between the twain. And that is more than most can do today. Separation from evil and from the wicked was before the man whose eyes the LORD had opened.

David viewed by revelation the divine doctrine and heavenly purpose of God in Christ Jesus, Psalm 139, and who is sufficient for these things? Without doubt they are hid from the wise and prudent. Nevertheless David saw them in spirit and much more besides.

He was a man of vision. O, not only were David's ears

bored, not only his heart melted, his spirit humbled, but his eyes were opened and illuminated by the radiance of the heavenly vision.

So it is with the seed of David, and to him shall the gathering of the people be. And no wonder. From whom else can they hear such things?

- He was a man of judgment.

David's eye did not pity the enemies of God and of his people. He rooted out from the promised land all those who destroyed the order and peace of God, of God's house, of God's inheritance, and of God's worshippers. He cut off the idolaters, drove out the uncircumcised, put the wicked to the sword, and ground to powder the sodomites.

Even in his extreme old age he knew how to exercise judgment on those who, after his decease, would assuredly arise and trouble Israel. In his prudence therefore he forewarned Solomon, admonishing him straitly how to deal with the enemies of God, of the peace of Israel, and of the government and worship of God's house.

Thus it was that David's judgment, even from the grave, arose to smite and cut off the haters of God. He being dead yet spake, and spake to the discovery and judgment

(i)   *Of Adonijah and his ambition.* He was slain in a moment, and good for the kingdom it was, else they had never been ruled by Solomon nor governed by the son of David. No more had God's house been built. Not by that ambitious place-seeker Adonijah. But Solomon built him an house. David saw all this beforehand. Though after the flesh his eyes failed, yet his judgment never diminished.

(ii) *Of Shimei and his covetousness.* He died the death of the wicked. Before his decease David laid a trap for this man's greed, who, hoping that Solomon's memory had failed along with David's dying counsel, in time walked right into it and was snared.

By such prudent and far-seeing judgments, plagues are stayed and godliness established. But it takes a man, a man like David, like Solomon, like the seed of David, to see it and have the courage to make and execute the judgment accordingly.

(iii) *Of Joab and his fierceness.* He was a mighty man, he loved David, but even more he loved war; he was at heart a mercenary, and after David's decease, was for sale.

For sale, because he did not value peace. He could not estimate Solomon, but rather chose to fight for Adonijah. But this unstable evaluation cost him his life. Now Solomon's name means, Peace. That, the man of war despised.

In the wisdom and vision of God David discerned Joab's heart. It was for war, and though all his life he fought the right battles, he fought them not because they must be fought but because he was a hard man, and no lover of the peace of God. David saw it by revelation and his dying counsel foresaw the end of the pitiless son of Zeruiah. Joab dug a pit for himself, and into it he fell.

Nevertheless he laid hold of the horns of the altar, choosing to die at the place of sacrifice. He begged no mercy from the executioner, but died like the brave man that he was. Who knows? Though he was put to the sword without mercy by David's judgment through Solomon, still he loved and served David and fell under the shadow of the altar of atonement.

Having delight in war he erred in not following David's chosen seed, and that was the fatal downfall of his cruel heart. David's judgment from the grave was justified in the issue, and Joab being skilled to war as he was, no doubt the judgment was salvation to Israel.

Thus the kingdom of peace was established in peace by David and his seed, being based upon the wise judgment of the king.

- He was a man of compassion.

Though not without that sternness, the lack of which would ensure that the kingdom must surely fall before the armies of the alien, David was also compassionate.

He sought out the paths and ways of mercy. Saith he, 'Is there yet any that is left of the house of Saul, that I may show him kindness for Jonathan's sake?' How he had wept at the death of Saul and Jonathan. How he cried and fasted for the dying infant.

David prayed for his enemies: 'They rewarded me evil for good to the spoiling of my soul. But as for me, when they were sick, my clothing was sackcloth: I humbled my soul with fasting; and my prayer returned into mine own bosom. I behaved myself as though he had been my friend or brother: I bowed down heavily, as one that mourneth for his mother.'

Only when they had proved incorrigible, despising David after he had shown himself merciful in the teeth of their hatred, I say, only after his enemies despised mercy, would David rise up in wrath.

But he was essentially compassionate. Judgment was a necessity for the establishment of the kingdom: but he himself was filled with compassion, he took no pleasure in destruction.

Of a truth David was pitiful and of great mercy, and so is his seed for ever.

This then is the humanity, and these are traits, seen in 'the seed of David according to the flesh.'

Now then, this is what we have observed in the first instance: David was a man.

Now consider:

¶ **NEXT, DAVID WAS AN HEIR.**

But of whom was he an heir? And of what?

Why, David was heir to Abraham, Matthew 1:1, 'The book of the generation of Jesus Christ, the son of David, *the son of Abraham.'*

Now then, if David is the son of Abraham then he is his heir. And if Jesus Christ is the son of David then that inheritance and David's also is his by right.

Wherefore it follows of necessity that Jesus Christ of the seed of David is heir to Abraham.

But what is that inheritance? Heir to what, precisely?

Why, of the promises. The promises of God. They were promised to Abraham and passed on to David and his seed for ever in an everlasting covenant, a new testament, confirmed by an immutable oath and sealed with the Holy Spirit of promise.

These promises originally made to Abraham were passed from heir to heir until David the king. In David they were expressed, enlarged, established and confirmed.

Nevertheless the inheritance remained no more than promises, still unfulfilled in fact, so that from David they passed each successive generation without being realised even until the coming of Christ.

Then what of all the heirs from David to Christ? And what about those from Abraham until David? This: 'These all died in faith, not having received the promises,' Hebrews 11:13.

But Jesus Christ, of the seed of David, and heir to Abraham, he received them. They are all his, all of them are fulfilled in him.

However, I inquire, Then what are these promises to Abraham, so prized by David and his seed? Basically two.

The first promise: That Abraham should have a son, and that his seed should be as the stars in the sky, the sand on the sea-shore, for multitude.

The second promise: That Abraham should inherit the land of promise.

Basically all the promises may be reduced to these two. However, since Abraham, each has been expanded and enlarged in successive Old Testament prophecies until it could appear that other promises must have been added, but this is not so.

It would have been impossible. Seen aright nothing more could have been promised, because no more could be given.

The entire plenitude of the riches of God for men is contained in the original, grand and comprehensive promises to Abraham. This is not my opinion or judgment. It is the apostolic revelation of the truth.

You can see that plainly from the Galatian epistle, the Hebrews, and Romans four in particular. It is one of the chief emphases of the New Testament. That is why it is implied in Paul's summary of the gospel concerning Jesus Christ the Son of God 'made' of the seed of David.

■ **The first promise:**

(of which David — hence his seed — is heir)

> That Abraham should have a son, and that
> his seed should be as the stars in the sky, the
> sand on the sea-shore, for multitude.

Now this promise of a son and a seed, though wonderfully gracious, may not seem so remarkable. But it is more than remarkable! And it is so for two reasons.

The first is this: Abraham was seventy-five years old when first he set foot in the land of promise, *then* he was promised a son. And as if that were not enough for faith — to expect a son at seventy-five years old — time passed, and the promise remained unfulfilled.

Ten years passed; Abraham was eighty-five. No son. Other ten years passed: ninety-five years old. Still no son. As if it were not enough to believe when one was seventy-five, what, when one was ninety-five? Still nothing.

Then where was the promise of God that Abraham should have a son?

Finally Abraham attained about one hundred years old,

and his body was as good as dead, his sap long, long dried out. What seed then could he give? He was as it were dead already. Not to mention his ancient wife Sarah, whose womb was dried up, barren, and as dead as Abraham's body.

Then where was the promise of God?

Certain and sure. For Abraham did have a son, Isaac by name, and at such a time. Moreover, Sarah herself received strength to conceive and bear the seed.

Now, although the promise of a son in itself considered may not seem so remarkable, once realise the circumstances in which Sarah bare Isaac to Abraham: then this is more than remarkable. It is downright miraculous.

The other reason that makes the promise to Abraham — of a son and a seed — more than remarkable, now follows.

The promise to Abraham that he should have a son and that his seed should be innumerable as the sand on the sea-shore was confirmed to Isaac in turn. Isaac also was heir to the promise. So the promise was to Abraham and his seed.

Moreover this promise passed also to Jacob. And went through Judah. In fact ultimately this inheritance of promises from God went even unto David, who was in the direct line of succession.

Nevertheless, what is extraordinary is this: when the promise was made to Abraham, and then to his son, Isaac, the word 'seed' was in the *singular*. Now this may not seem so remarkable, but consider what the apostle has to say about it:

'Now to Abraham and his seed
were the promises made.
He saith not'
— God saith not —
'And to seeds, as of many;
but as of one,
And to thy seed,
*which is Christ!'*

*Galatians 3:16.*

**Then who was the real heir to the promises?**

Isaac, Jacob, the children of Israel, David? No, for they were many, and 'He saith not, And to seeds, as of many; but as of one, And to thy seed,' singular. That *one* is the heir.

I tell you, one is the heir. Christ is the heir, his is the inheritance, and of him, Isaac the son of Abraham, and Jacob with the children of Israel, were but the figures!

What a wonderful truth this is, how much it stands at the heart of apostolic preaching, such an integral part of the true gospel that no preaching of the gospel is complete without it. Here is the essence of New Testament revelation: marvellous!

What we are being taught is this: although Isaac was born to Abraham and Sarah so miraculously that it appeared as if he were actually the promised seed himself, what transpired is that he was not.

He could not be, that is obvious, because Isaac himself received the same promise about that future seed as did his father before him. Then of necessity he was not the seed, but — with Abraham — a co-heir to God's promise of a seed.

From which it follows that there is a depth to the promise of God not apparent on face value. Certainly Abraham, Isaac and Jacob were heirs. But what unfolds is this: there is a second and more profound meaning to the use of the word 'heir'. It is this: they were heirs to *the* heir.

If then Isaac himself was not that son or seed of Abraham intended in the counsels of God by the promise — but only another step towards that seed — what then was his personal significance?

Much every way. Chiefly that he was heir to the promise.

That the promise was of *the* heir, did not make Isaac's privilege any less honourable. It is an astounding honour to be an heir to the Heir himself.

Not least significant in Isaac is that — despite being the immediate and literal son of Abraham — he was the first to show that a long line of chosen generations must pass before the actual Seed and Son of Abraham according to the counsels of God should be born.

A succession of the elect should pass on that promise by inheritance from Abraham through Isaac, till the seed himself should come of the same line.

Yes, Isaac was distinctive in every way. But he was most distinctive as a figure of him that was to come.

Consider this distinction. I do not mean to consider Isaac as a type of Christ throughout his lifetime; wonderful as that is, particularly at Mount Moriah. But consider him in the context of his birth and the promises.

Consider that Isaac — regarded as Abraham's promised child — depicted Jesus Christ the true Son and Heir of Abraham and the promises in three ways:

*Firstly.*

He was himself a child of promise. GOD promised this child, this seed, and promised him to Abraham through Sarah.

But before Abraham was, Jesus Christ was promised from the dawn of time in the garden of Eden. There it is written, Genesis 3:15, The seed of the woman would bruise the head of the serpent, and the serpent would bruise the heel of the seed of the woman.

That is, that the child of promise should stamp out the serpent and his seed, but that the stamping would cost him dearly. Well, 'It pleased the LORD to bruise him,' but in so doing, Satan's head was crushed and forthwith he was bound as with a great chain and imprisoned that he should deceive the nations no more.

This prophecy of the seed of the woman, his bruising, and the effect of it, was before Abraham existed; before the flood.

Now, for all the remarkable and even miraculous providences attending Isaac's life, can it possibly be supposed that he was the fulfilment of this ancient and venerable prophecy? Certainly not. A far more remarkable life, and an even more miraculous testimony, would be needed before the wise would concede that!

In any event, the central part of the Genesis prophecy respects the crushing of Satan's head, power and dominion, at the expense of the heel of the seed of the woman. But what did Isaac ever stamp out? Whom caused he to fall from heaven? And whenever was his heel bruised?

Then of whom does the Genesis 3:15 prophecy speak?

It signified exactly the same seed of the woman, or seed of promise, as did Isaac himself. It signified one to come. Both promises — the prophecy and the child — spake of the seed of promise. Both speak of Christ.

Besides, that Isaac was a figure of the divinely appointed son of Abraham is evident. For had Isaac himself been the son whom God meant in that promise, then the promises would have ceased thereafter. But after Isaac, far from ceasing, they continued increasing till the coming of Christ. Then they ceased.

Nevertheless, hundreds of years before they ceased, and thousands of years after Isaac died, the great evangelical prophet Isaiah cried in vision at the future sight of the long-distant advent of Christ and says of that one who was to come,

'Unto us a child is born,
Unto us a son is given.'

*Isaiah 9:6.*

91

Of whom spake he? Certainly not deceased Isaac. He had been dead these thousands of years. Then whom? Why, of the future seed of the woman, the coming son of Abraham, the singular seed of promise, none other than Jesus Christ the Son of God,

'made of the seed of David according to the flesh.'

This suffices to comment on the first way in which Isaac depicted the true son of Abraham: both were children of promise through the patriarch Abraham. The promises of God preceded their birth. However the one was but a figure of the other.

*Secondly.*

Isaac depicted Christ in his birth. For, in a figure, Isaac was not conceived after the flesh.

The sign of circumcision given by God to Abraham before the conception of Isaac signified that the natural, fleshly, mode of conception did not apply.

It signified that, it was not really so. It was a sign showing that, if not in reality then in a figure, Isaac was born of Sarah without human agency.

This figure showed that the son of Abraham was not conceived according to nature but according to God. Not conceived according to the flesh but according to the Spirit. Not conceived according to normal processes but according to miraculous intervention.

Because the sign of circumcision implied that, as to

paternal parentage, the flesh had been taken out of sight, removed from view, in Abraham. Of course it is but a figure. But God did not give it for nothing.

Nevertheless, whether figure, picture, sign or not, it was still true in fact that Isaac himself was conceived — however miraculous that conception in view of his parents' age — from the fusion of the natural fleshly seed of Abraham with the natural fleshly seed of Sarah. That is, although by divinely aided, still by natural processes. Moreover that this conception — however divinely assisted — took place according to nature, to the natural fleshly order of events.

Abraham's prior circumcision made no difference to that.

Then why circumcision? It was a sign. A figure not of the birth of the child promised to him as his immediate heir, but of the birth of that Child of promise ultimately promised to him as the Heir of God.

That child was Christ. And, saith the prophet, calling out to humanity in the midst of time:

'A virgin shall conceive,
and bear a son,
and shall call his name
Immanuel.'

*Isaiah 7:14.*

Now all this came to pass in Jesus Christ, who was 'made' of the seed of David according to the flesh.

And when this came to pass, what we see is that all

93

figures, types, shadows, prophecies, are simply eclipsed by the superlative nature of the event!

For example, take Abraham's circumcision, a figure showing that the flesh was not involved in the conception of Isaac. A figure. A symbol. A sign of the birth of Abraham's son according to the promise of God.

But the thing figured, the reality symbolised, the substance foreshadowed, showed that there was no paternal human agency involved *at all*, no male seed whatsoever, no father after the flesh existed, in the birth of Jesus Christ the Son of God.

Nevertheless, however eclipsed by the event, the figure at least dimly showed, The seed of promise should not be born after the flesh.

*Thirdly.*

The third way in which Isaac — considered as Abraham's promised child — depicted Jesus Christ as the true son and heir of Abraham and the promises now follows:

It is this: Isaac signified Christ in that he was both begotten and received from the dead in a figure.

What figure?

That figure when 'Abraham considered not his own body, now dead.' Dead. That is it, 'now dead.' Before Isaac was conceived. 'Neither yet the deadness of Sarah's womb.' There it is also, 'deadness.' Before through faith also Sarah herself received strength to conceive seed. Then, what summed her up was 'deadness.'

Now out of these conditions Isaac was conceived and brought forth. Out of the dead. Out of a twofold testimony to deadness. In a figure. And out of such conditions Abraham's true son and heir was promised in fact.

However, there is all the difference between the one set forth by that figure and the figure itself. For if in a figure Isaac was begotten from the dead, then in reality

> 'Jesus Christ of the seed of David
> *was* raised from the dead'
> — no figure about it —
> 'according to my gospel.'

As to Isaac, these things happened unto him as a promise never realised in fact. Otherwise, had he been brought forth from the dead as a verity, how was it that afterwards he both died and was gathered to his fathers?

But to Jesus Christ, raised from the dead according to my gospel, these things happened to him as a real experience in truth.

'Christ being raised from the dead dieth no more; death hath no more dominion over him.' Though once he tasted death, he was raised from it by the glory of the Father, and now his is the power of an endless life.

Jesus Christ is now 'declared to be the Son of God with power, according to the spirit of holiness, by the resurrection from the dead.' Therefore the promise to Abraham, the sure mercies of David, all these figures pertaining to the Heir, are intended to be seen in and identified with

> 'Jesus Christ,
> come of the seed of David according to the flesh.'

But besides Isaac, Jacob his son also set forth the true and singular 'seed' of Abraham. It was in Jacob, the grandson of Abraham, that 'the sand of the sea-shore' and 'the stars in the sky for multitude' became a potential.

Hence it is written, 'The God of Abraham, the God of Isaac, and the God of Jacob.' A sequence is entailed to convey the whole truth.

Jacob — whose name was changed to Israel — bore sons. They were called 'the children of Israel.' That is what distinguished Jacob. His seed became as innumerable as the sand upon the sea-shore.

But this too was a figure of him that was to come, the true seed of promise, of the divinely intended son of Abraham.

First Abraham received the promise of a seed not born after the flesh. Then Isaac showed that seed beyond the reach and power of death. Finally, in continuity, Jacob — or Israel — depicted the fruitfulness of Christ risen from the grave in terms of sonship.

For when Christ rose, the Spirit of life was given. Sons were born, the children of God multiplied. An innumerable company, as the sand on the sea-shore and the stars in the heaven for multitude, was brought to life and sonship by Jesus Christ, the Son of God, raised from the dead.

Thus the promise is fulfilled — in Christ — of a great multitude whom no man can number. And yet the truth still holds good, *the seed is singular.* It remains singular. As found in Christ, and Christ in us, the saints all can say, 'I live; yet not I, but Christ liveth in me.'

By that indwelling, by the Holy Ghost, by the grace of God, by the Father in heaven, we can look upon that untold myriad clothed in white, with palms in their hands, and say of a truth,

'That seed was Christ.'

Now all this, and no less, you are intended to see and understand by the essential gospel truth conveyed by the word

'made of the seed of David according to the flesh.'

Why David? Because David was a man, as we have shown. But also because David was an heir.

As to that inheritance of which he was heir, in essence it stands for the two great promises of God to Abraham.

I have finished my brief explanation of the first promise concerning a son and a seed. Now I turn to the second great promise, given to Abraham, and preserved in David. It is that to which the divinely appointed Son and Seed is heir.

■ The second promise:

That Abraham should inherit
the land of promise.

This refers to the country of the Canaanites, the land of Israel. But the truth is, Abraham never inherited that land.

One may say, But his seed did, when Joshua led the

tribes into the promised land and divided it for an inheritance for ever.

For ever? Then what of the frequent alien recapture of the whole or part of that land with the consequent servitude of the children of Israel? That happened many times under the judges, under Saul, and even until David.

If one will say, But the land had rest under David and Solomon. Then what of the revolt of the ten tribes against the house of David, no sooner had Solomon died?

For ever? What about the collapse of the kingdom with the fall of Samaria? What about the ten tribes being lost and dispossessed by the Assyrians for ever? And the heathen occupying their inheritance?

What about the Assyrian and Babylonian conquest of the land? What about the captivity in Babylon of the only two remaining tribes?

What about the subsequent occupations, the four hundred dark years between Malachi and Matthew, the Roman conquest? And what, I pray, what for the last two thousand years?

If one says, But the Jews are back now. I reply, That is a conjecture: not one of them can show their genealogy from the original stock of the children of Israel. Yet the one thing required on the Jews' return to the land under Ezra and Nehemiah was that a Jew must show his genealogy and actually be placed in the chronicles of the tribes of Israel.

Now, nobody knows their tribe, even supposing that

they might be of the twelve tribes. Now, Sephardim or Ashkenazim is the most they can hope for. But no tribes were called after those names.

There is no proof whatsoever that the people calling themselves Jews today — practising a hopelessly compromised and deviant departure from the pure law required under the Old Covenant — no proof whatsoever that they are of the twelve tribes. There is only claim. Not proof. There can be no proof. There are no records.

Moreover it follows therefore that in no way can the people calling themselves Jews today reclaim that inheritance originally divided by lot to the twelve tribes under Joshua. Because — even if they were descended from the scattered remnant — no one would know where to go, because *not one* knows either his tribe or its lot beyond wishful thinking and wistful surmise.

Not only is it impossible to trace the ten tribes, but also the line of descent to the Jews — Judah and Benjamin — is utterly broken, fragmented, and lost in the mists of time.

All that exists today is a people calling themselves Jews, practising a corrupted form of that Judaism which already had submerged the scriptures beneath a flood of puerile interpretations from the Rabbis and tradition of the elders, over two thousand years ago.

Besides that a mixed multitude occupies much the same land today — with only a small percentage of these having any religious profession — what possible consolation can that be to the many generations of Jews and would-be Jews who have died beforehand, never having set foot in the land?

For ever?

For ever? Yet the promise was to Abraham and his seed for ever.

Now, whatever anyone argues about what happened under Joshua to those tribes actually led by him into the land. Ignoring for the moment what I have pointed out as having happened since that time. Leaving aside for the sake of argument the facts of the last two thousand years: It still remains that Abraham *himself* never inherited.

For the promise was to Abraham and his seed for ever.

In fact Abraham inherited not so much as a foot's breadth. Come to that, neither did Isaac nor Jacob. Furthermore not one of the original children of Israel owned so much as a few square feet of land to pitch his tent upon.

So what is this about for ever?

The truth is that Abraham, far from for ever, *never* inherited the land of Canaan. And yet certainly it was promised to him and his seed.

Then of course it follows, as in the case of the first promise to Abraham, that a deeper, more profound and spiritual meaning was intended in the promise of God than appears on face value. And without this true interpretation everything becomes both contradictory and chaotic, as, for example, in the fantastic dispensational and premillennial notions.

Evidently a deeper purpose was intended in the promise,

and this all the New Testament writers consistently teach. For example, Hebrews 11:9,

'By faith
Abraham sojourned
in the land of promise,
as in a strange country,
dwelling in tabernacles
with Isaac and Jacob,
the heirs with him
of the same promise.'

And what same promise was this? The promise that he should inherit the land. But the writer is pointing out, neither Abraham, Isaac nor Jacob ever did inherit the land.

To the contrary, Abraham 'sojourned' — but one dwells, not sojourns, in an inheritance. Abraham was in a strange country — but this was the land promised to him as his: yet the writer says 'a strange country.' Abraham dwelt in tents, tabernacles — but one builds buildings, one lays the foundations of one's house, in the land of one's inheritance. However, this was not true of Abraham.

Nor Isaac and Jacob, Abraham's son and grandson. In tents with Abraham in a strange country.

But if one viewed the promise of the land superficially — as do the premillennialists — then these things, my brethren, ought not so to be! Abraham should have dwelt in a familiar country, builded his house, and passed on all by inheritance first to Isaac then to Jacob.

To the contrary, like itinerant nomads, the ancient Abraham, with his son and grandson, passed through a strange country, in which even the old grandfather had as yet no inheritance. But now it was time to pass the inheritance from his son to his grandson!

From the youngest at some fifteen years old through to the oldest at some one hundred and seventy-five, they had not so much land as a grave to bury their dead. Abraham gained not a foot's breadth, nor did Isaac, nor Jacob, nor his twelve sons.

Then what of the promise? Well, it follows: obviously this promise must be viewed spiritually.

And so it was: 'By faith Abraham sojourned in the land of promise.' Then faith was the way in which Abraham viewed the promise. And since it was made to him, who are we to view it any differently? He viewed it *spiritually;* by faith. So did Isaac. And Jacob. That is what it says:

> 'These all died in faith,
> not having received the promises,
> but confessed that they were
> strangers and pilgrims
> on the earth.'

Not only was it true that the patriarchs did not inherit the land as a matter of record, but they could not inherit it as a matter of fact.

They could not inherit this second promise of the land of Canaan literally because — as we have seen — the deeper, divine and spiritual meaning of the first promise entailed resurrection from the dead.

Now, resurrection does not respect time nor has it to do

with this present world. Resurrection respects eternity and it has to do with the world to come. But when that comes, this world — and Canaan with it — will have passed away.

In that world, there are no seas, no boundaries, no separate nations or countries. It is a new earth. Then there is no Canaan there. Well, to be precise, it is all Canaan there. Nothing but 'the land of promise' is there. The whole of that earth is the true Canaan of rest.

Precisely because the figure of resurrection is seen to convey the real meaning of the first promise, so it follows of necessity that the real meaning of the second promise — that Abraham should inherit the land — must likewise be conveyed by a figure.

And why should it seem a thing incredible with you that God, who raises the dead, should bring in the world to come for those dead whom he has raised?

Given — and it must be given — that the first promise speaks of Christ risen and the heirs of Christ raised in him. Granted, that this is the true spiritual view intended of God in the first promise to Abraham. Accepted, that the patriarchs believed this at the beginning, as the apostles interpreted it at the end.

Then it follows: the second promise cannot be interpreted more literally than the first. Both must be interpreted with equal spirituality, the second as the first. Moreover, the second promise rests upon the first; and if the one entailed the resurrection then the other must respect the glory.

And so Abraham saw it.

Abraham understood this: he died in faith, a thing impossible had he expected to inherit whilst he was yet alive. If that were the case, he would have died in frustrated bitterness; but he did not, he died in faith.

Then he must have expected to rise from the dead. If so, he must have expected to inherit the earth in the world to come. And so it is written of him:

> 'They that say such things declare plainly
> that they *seek* a country.'

But he was in Canaan: how could he have sought it? If in the land of promise he still sought for another country he declares plainly that he looks on *that* as an earthly token, just as he looked on *Isaac* as a fleshly token, of better things to come. So it was he sought not Israel below but the heavenly country above.

> 'But now they desire a better country,
> that is, an heavenly.'

A better country than the earthly land of promise. The heavenly land of glory. That was what Abraham believed about the promise, and therefore, having inherited nothing in this present world, still he could die in faith. Of course: all his expectation lay beyond the grave and in the world to come. And thus he understood the promise.

Just as he understood the first promise. Abraham saw clearly that Isaac was but a figure of Christ and not the substance. Jesus said, Abraham rejoiced to see my day, and was glad. If so, the patriarch would have made no mistake about Isaac, but would have looked through him to the ultimate promised seed.

In like manner Abraham discerned the second promise. He saw clearly that Canaan was but a figure of the world to come and not the substance. Therefore he looked through Canaan to the heavenly country beyond. And so did Isaac and Jacob. These all

'Confessed
that they were strangers and pilgrims
on the earth.'

The earth? Well, that earth in particular called the land of Canaan. First, they saw the figure and looked for the Son who should bring in a better resurrection. Next, they saw the figure and looked for the Son who should bring in a better inheritance.

They looked, they looked, and they died looking. And the Son of God being come of the seed of David according to the flesh, he shall not disappoint them.

He shall answer all their faith and raise their dust to immortality at the last day.

At his appearing and kingdom in glory they shall inherit the earth; the world is theirs. And an earth and world incomparably beyond anything this present scene could ever envisage.

With good cause — these ages past — their flesh doth rest in hope. Because hope maketh not ashamed, for one has now come who has abolished death and brought life and immortality to light through the gospel. He is Abraham's seed and the true heir of the promises made to Abraham.

These were the two ancient promises of which we have

spoken, being given in figures, on the one hand of Isaac begotten out of the dead, and on the other of inheritance in the land of Canaan.

By these was signified in the first place the reality of the Son of God declared by the resurrection from the dead, and in the second place the inheritance which is to be interpreted according to this sound doctrine.

For so the apostle Paul commands our faith, saying:

'For the promise,'

that is, the second promise to Abraham. Literally the inheritance of Canaan. But by the faith of Abraham spiritually discerned as a coming world beyond the judgment. And so Paul teaches the church of God in the epistle to the Romans:

'For the promise,
*that he should be the heir of the world.'*

Mark that well. That is how Paul actually reads the second promise to Abraham. Therefore, that is what it means. To continue:

'For the promise,
that he should be the heir of the world,
was not to Abraham, or to his seed,
through the law,
but through the righteousness of faith.'

*Romans 4:13.*

Now, that seed — singular — is Christ. But when shall

Christ inherit the world? When Abraham does. Albeit Abraham shall inherit for no other reason than that he is heir to the Heir, and hence to the Heir's inheritance.

But when shall Christ inherit?

This true Heir, this Son of David, the Son of Abraham, when shall he inherit? He shall inherit according to the laws of inheritance: after death, and after change of possession.

After death? Well, he shall inherit in the resurrection from the dead, and in the resurrection in the last day.

After change of possession? He shall inherit when this present world itself has changed beyond recognition after the great conflagration in the terrible day of judgment.

> 'For the earth and the works that are therein
> shall be burned up,
> and the elements
> shall melt with fervent heat.'

Here is the change of possession. When this world has gone through the fiery deluge, when the world to come has come to pass, then.

Then shall the son of David the son of Abraham, the risen heir, the Son of God, with all the true seed, all in Christ, all the Israel of God, then shall he come into that world promised to him through Abraham, and more, promised to him before this world was.

Then. Then shall be the consummation, the kingdom, the power and the glory, world without end. Amen.

107

Now this promise, the second promise to Abraham, also passed to David, is intended to be understood and conveyed by the words:

'made of the seed of David according to the flesh.'

Because, as we have shown, David was an heir.

That is, the heir of the promises made unto his father Abraham, and passed by inheritance to the one in whom all is fulfilled: Jesus Christ, the Son of God and seed of David.

Of whom we have many things to say, and hard to be uttered. But what we have said is not hard to be uttered. That is simple. Clear and plain. It is the unadulterated apostolic gospel.

Many things to say, but now, chiefly, that we see in David the truth prefigured. Truth that respects his greater son. Truth that commands our faith. Truth that declares,

primarily, that DAVID WAS A MAN.
But also, that DAVID WAS AN HEIR.

That he was an heir, and whose heir, and of what inheritance, we have made abundantly clear. For it must be made clear, because — despite the present climate of tolerated apathetic ignorance — in New Testament terms all this is simple and essential gospel truth.

However, to continue to the third and last main feature discerned in David. It is this: DAVID WAS A KING. Which I now proceed to expound.

## ¶  LAST, DAVID WAS A KING.

David was a king in three ways:

> He was a prophetic king.
> He was a priestly king.
> He was an absolute king.

In the first place then,

- David was a prophetic king.

David shows that in the mind of God the gift of prophecy is not to be distinct from the majesty of kingship.

To the contrary, in the purpose of God the insight that makes the prophet prophetic and the character that makes the king royal merge and blend in the vision of one majestic person, *the Messiah*, of whom David was the type or figure.

How important this is! Remember that Jesus Christ came of the seed of David, admonishes the apostle; never forget. So important that Christ himself willingly accepts the title 'Son of David' in the gospels.

And why not? For we can see prefigured in David — and nowhere else so clearly — the truth of the manhood of Jesus Christ.

His is a kingly manhood. And the king is the prophet. Yes, The prophet. Of him Moses wrote to Israel in old time, 'The Lord thy God will raise up unto thee a Prophet from the midst of thee.'

And, saith God, 'This is my beloved Son: hear him.' And these words spake he on the holy mount, even as he obscured from the apostolic and gospel view the fading glory of Moses and Elijah, the prophets of the Old Covenant.

What then were Moses and Elijah? But figures of the true. Yet not such clear figures as David. For David was a kingly prophet, and by so much, better depicted Christ.

This the scriptures teach and the Jews acknowledged, John 7:42, 'Hath not the scripture said, That Christ cometh of the seed of David, and out of the town of Bethlehem, where David was?' And when he comes, 'He shall tell us all things.' And why not? God's king is God's prophet.

His is the ultimate speech. All the former prophets were provisional by comparison. Hebrews 1:1, 'God, who at sundry times and in divers manners spake in time past unto the fathers by the prophets, hath in these last days spoken unto us by his Son.'

He is the truth. Actually the truth itself. Not only truthful: the truth. The truth is in Jesus. All truth, even about created things, the creation itself. 'All things were made by him; and without him was not any thing made that was made.'

Every fact, material or abstract, relates to him. The truth as regards the revelation of God, his nature and purpose, is in him. No truth but what originates in him, returns to him, and is measured by him. When he speaks, it is ultimate.

See that ye refuse not him that speaketh. He is God's

final speech. Nothing has been said, nothing is being said, nothing will be said, as regards the truth, but that this Word is the final and authoritative Speaker.

The prophet. A royal prophet. His utterances are majestic. Absolute. Nothing can be added. Nothing can be taken away. There is no subject permissible but that his is the last word upon it.

Creation itself came from the word of his mouth. Providence is subject to his speech. He upholds all things by the word of his power. His voice shall raise the dead, his shout dissolve the universe.

The truth is, ultimately, that there is nothing worth hearing but what comes from his lips. No one worth hearing save his exclusive person. Every other worth is relative. Relative to him. Relative to his word. Relative to his speech. 'In the beginning was the Word, and the Word was with God, and the Word was God.'

Royal decree, absolute final authority, is in him. His is the speech from the throne. Consummate upon every subject, the fame of his wisdom sounds from afar. If the half had not been told of Solomon's wisdom, what shall be said of this seed of David?

First depicted in the prophetic king, no wonder Jesus himself asks, Mark 2:25, 'Have ye never read what David did?' What did he do? Much every way. And this also: King David depicted Messiah's prophetic utterance as the final speech of God; God's last word to men; his utterance is by the voice of the king. David showed it.

Saith Christ, 'David himself said by the Holy Ghost.'

That was David the king's way of saying things: By the Holy Ghost. And this is pure prophecy. Saith Peter the apostle, 'The Holy Ghost by the mouth of David spake.' So then, David spake by the Holy Ghost on the one hand, and the Holy Ghost spake by the mouth of David on the other.

And what shall I more say? No purer divinity exists than this. After this, there is nothing to debate, argue, interpret, question, or compare with others. It is, Thus saith the Lord. God has spoken; let all mortal flesh keep silence.

David was a visionary prophet. Acts 2:25, 'David speaketh concerning Christ.' But he was some one thousand years before Christ. Then how spake he concerning him? Because of what he saith in another place, 'I foresaw the Lord always before my face.' He foresaw, he saw Christ before. That is, a thousand years before.

No wonder Peter comments upon David, 'Therefore being a prophet ...'

David was a noble prophet. Acts 2:30, 'Therefore being a prophet, and knowing that God had sworn with an oath to him, that of the fruit of his loins, according to the flesh, he would raise up Christ to sit on his throne.' Therefore he did homage to the One that should come. Noble, he delighted to give the glory to the coming Messiah, with all his heart and breath. 'David speaketh concerning him.'

A kingly prophet, and one who depicted Christ in a unique way. He set forth the manhood of the Son of God come of the seed of David according to the flesh. Kingly manhood, and although declared in the resurrection, nevertheless foreseen in prophecy. 'David seeing this before, spake of the resurrection of Christ,' Acts 2:31.

And if that be said of the figure, what of the true? David foresaw the Lord. Then what did the Lord himself foresee? The end of Judaism. The end of the Old Covenant. The end of the age. The end of the world. For this is what he teaches in Matthew 24, Mark 13, and Luke 21. The 'little apocalypse' as it is called.

The Book of the Revelation he foresees. 'The revelation of Jesus Christ, which God gave unto him' is the title of this book. He foresaw, you see. He foresaw the dreadful day of judgment, the destruction and punishment of the disobedient, their everlasting torment. He foresaw the holy city, the bride, the assembly, the world to come, the saints in glory, the everlasting bliss.

Consider: If David foresaw, then how much more the Messiah? For David foreshadowed Christ.

Wherefore the apostle speaking by the Holy Ghost declares, 'I have found David the son of Jesse, a man after mine own heart.' And why saith he this in the word of the Lord? Because a man after God's own heart is one who of necessity must possess visionary insight, the divinity of the seer, the prophetic boldness. Without these things there is no correspondence with the heart of God. But David had these things.

Hence God 'by the mouth of his servant David spake.' Yes, but now David is dead, buried, and gathered to his fathers, his sepulchre being with us to this day.

Nevertheless, in his seed 'I will build again the tabernacle of David.' That is, God will raise up the house of David for ever, by the resurrection of his seed from the dead, even Jesus Christ, the royal prophet, the Messiah who tells us all things, the Alpha and Omega, the faithful and true witness.

David saw inwardly with the mystic penetration of the seer. He looked not upon the things which can be seen, but upon things unseen, things eternal. He knew that things seen were but temporal. He did not regard carnal Israel, seeing after the flesh. He saw the true seed of Abraham, the Israel of God. As to Israel after the flesh, 'let their table become a snare.'

David did not look at worldly types and shadows, carnal forms and figures, outward signs and ordinances, as if they were anything. They were nothing. The reality was everything, lending a brief meaning, a fading glory, to external figures, types, ceremonies, and passing forms.

David looked past the types and shadows, through the signs and ordinances, to the unseen, to reality, to the very substance itself, to the essence of things divine and spiritual.

He looked through Jerusalem to the heavenly city. Through the temple to the house of God not made with hands. He looked through the literal seed of Israel to the spiritual children of Abraham. He looked through the earthly Canaan to the heavenly land of promise.

David looked, and looked from within, and looked for a new Jerusalem, a holy city from God out of heaven, a world to come of everlasting glory, a kingdom of God which stood not in meat and drink and carnal ordinances but in righteousness, peace and joy in the Holy Ghost.

He looked, I say, not at the things which can be seen, for the things which can be seen are temporal. He looked at things unseen, things visionary, things divine. And in this way David foreshadowed the Word of life.

David was a prophet, as it is written in the Hebrews, 'Of David also, and Samuel, and of the prophets.' And all these spake of Christ till he came. As to that coming, 'God limiteth a certain day, saying in David.' Saying in David, you observe. David spoke God's mind. And he spoke because he saw. As he himself said, 'I believed, therefore have I spoken.'

David saw; he had the sight. He had vision; he saw unseen things. He made out the future; he was a seer. 'So also is Christ.' The Son of God 'made of the seed of David according to the flesh.' It must be so: a man after God's own heart must be a seer. Then how much Christ sees. So much the more.

Even so, how much David saw. He looked into the sky with dimming eyes that did not see it, and in the visions of God saw Christ ascended into the heavens a thousand years or ever he came into the world. A thousand years.

With inturned sight David looked out across the centuries and saw. He saw; he felt himself translated in time, transported in space; he felt himself outside the city wall an entire millennium into the future. He looked; he saw them there; he felt; he cried, 'They part my garments among them, and cast lots upon my vesture.'

A thousand years later, on that spot, they did precisely to his seed what David in a trance then saw and felt done to him. In Christ it came to pass.

David saw. David felt. In the solitary watches he felt the agonising impalement tear at his palms and soles, lacerating and ripping and crushing through skin, flesh, muscle, sinew and bone. He felt, and as one who could bear no longer, no longer contain such sickening pain, he cried out, 'They pierced my hands and my feet!' But they did not. Awakening as a man out of deep sleep, amazed, he viewed his skin intact; his hands unbruised; his feet unblemished.

But a thousand years hence there was no awakening, no remission: it was a reality to the seed of David according to the flesh.

David's ears were open; 'Mine ear hast thou bored.' He heard voices call out in the night seasons; he heard voices cry out in cruel mockery. Suspended, he seemed suspended; he seemed to look down, all outstretched, from the pierced heights of God-forsaken rejection.

'He trusted on the LORD, that he would deliver him.' The noises drummed at his ears. Like the pack they bayed; like dogs they barked; they hounded him with their voices: 'Let him deliver him, seeing he delighted in him.' But there was no deliverance.

No; no deliverance in the dream. 'For God speaketh once, yea twice, yet man perceiveth it not. In a dream, in a vision of the night, when deep sleep falleth upon men, in slumberings upon the bed; then he openeth the ears of men, and sealeth their instruction.' No deliverance.

O my God, I cry in the daytime, but thou hearest not; and in the night season, and am not silent. Our fathers trusted in thee, and thou didst deliver them.

If so, then, 'Let him deliver him,' mock the howling pack, and the rising chorus as the rulers bay 'Aha, aha.' That. And, 'Yea, mine own familiar friend, in whom I trusted, which did eat of my bread, hath lifted up his heel against me.' 'I am a worm, and no man: a reproach of men, and despised of the people.' That, too. But worst, infinitely worst of all, 'My God, my God, why hast thou forsaken me?'

Much more: in a storm of prophetic passion, all wrung with pain, drenched with sweat, David cried, torn to the bowels, 'My God, my God, why hast thou forsaken me?' He panted, he cried. As pants the hart for the water brooks, he gasped, his moisture dried up within him. But 'they gave me gall for my meat, and in my thirst they gave me vinegar to drink.'

So they did, as David's vision of agony untold looked down from the impaled heights near one thousand years before the time.

Then waked he, as one aroused out of sleep; David came to himself, and lo, it was a dream. And David was as one that awakeneth, he openeth the eyes, and behold, he sat in his place alone. And he perceived that he had seen a vision. 'My God, my God, why hast thou forsaken me?' he had cried out with a dark and shuddering horror from his very soul, but when he came to himself, there was no cause.

No cause. No cause for centuries to come. No cause in David. No, because it was a vision; it was prophecy. 'The Holy Ghost spake by the mouth of David.' And not without cost to David. Nevertheless it was but a vision; he had fallen into a trance.

But not so in Christ. In Christ it was the reality. No

dream, no awakening, no trance. The reality came to pass in Christ, come of the seed of David according to the flesh.

David, I say, David was a prophet. He was a seer. He saw in visions of the night. His ear was opened. And, wondrous as was this divine and spiritual insight of the king, yet it was as nothing, it was but a shadow, it was as if the half had not been told, as compared with the fulfilment, the substance, the plenitude of Christ himself.

And yet consider the richness of David's utterance! Consider the Psalms of David.

What sadness, what pathos, what joy, what ecstasy, what a vast experience is encompassed. How profound the depths plumbed, how lofty the heights scaled, how expansive the area covered.

Such feeling for the universe, such sympathy with creation, such sensitivity towards nature, such accord with heaven and earth. Such rapport we find, with sea and dry land, rivers and floods, trees and deserts, mountains and hills; with beasts and fowl, cattle and dragons of the deep, fish of the sea, with every living thing, with all that hath breath in earth and sky and sea.

How rich David's insight into and awareness of manhood before God; how perceptive his sense of destiny; how elevated his view of humanity; how inward his appreciation of character. David's perception could indeed pierce to the dividing asunder of soul and spirit, joints and marrow, and discern the thoughts and intents of the heart. Wot ye not that such a man as he can certainly divine?

And what intuitive quickness he had of all that was

spiritual; what divinity was his; what awareness of God. He perceived divine persons, was subject to the divine work, and worshipped God alone.

Hear, O Israel; The Lord our God is one Lord: and thou shalt love the Lord thy God with all thy heart, and with all thy soul, and with all thy mind, and with all thy strength. And David did. All the days of his life.

What a seeing of the paths of the Lord, the ways of God, all the days of his life. What a looking into the grave, into sheol, beyond it, to the resurrection, the ascension, the glory. What perception of Christ's ministry from the glory, the Spirit's administration below, of God over all blessed for evermore. What soul-transporting views had he of the righteous judgment executed, of sights even unto Mount Zion, of new Jerusalem, of the land that is very far off, of the king in his beauty, even unto the world to come whereof we speak.

This was David. All, all this was and is true of David.

Yet of his seed, he is but the shadow. No more than a pale reflection. Believe it: the half hath not been told thee.

How reverent David was! How seriously he took the house of God, its service, priesthood, and worship. How precious the unity of the brethren to David. How sweet the concord, the united assembly of God's people.

How experimental David was in the Spirit. How deeply led into all truth; how well versed with the word, words, statutes, judgments, commandments, precepts, counsels, the law and testimony of the Lord.

He was not a man with a brittle crust of selected texts which when broken revealed vanity and emptiness beneath. He was all scripture right through, woven warp, woof and fibre into his inmost being. He thought scripture, felt it, willed it, lived it, was it: not only was he wrapped about and encompassed with scripture, he was packed solid with the word of God all the way to the core: neither lightness nor vanity dwelt in David.

Solid packed, God's word his meat day and night, yet experimentally moved by the Holy Ghost alone. This was David's matter, and so it is with his seed for ever: full, but full, of the Holy Ghost.

All this conspired to elevate the manhood of David and ennoble his humanity way above, soaring above ordinary men. Yet he humbled himself greatly to those of low degree. Of great humility of mind, he regarded the poor. What a stature: he towered above the mediocre! Above all others, save him whom he prefigured.

David; disciplined in the school of God, taught by the Spirit, instructed by Christ, full of holy doctrine, packed to the depths with the word of God experimentally learned. David. David, I say, was manhood personified.

In David manhood is realised, fulfilled, achieved, and magnified to its utmost. It reaches to all bounds, every perimeter, cultivated to the full and abundantly fruitful.

Look at his history! Observe his writings! See his ability! Number his talents! Perceive his devotion! Mark his integrity! Behold his meekness! And say, Lo, Zion, thy King cometh unto thee, meek and lowly, and riding upon an ass, and upon a colt the foal of an ass.

Manhood personified. Behold the man. No wonder it is said, 'I have found David the son of Jesse, a man after mine own heart.' A man perfectly developed. Human nature really suited to God. This is he of whose loins, according to the flesh, Christ came.

Yet consider this: Like his seed, he never even went to school! From a child the one kept the sheep of Jesse, and the other the shop of Joseph. The one was an uneducated shepherd, and the other an unschooled carpenter. Now mark it: *God alone developed this manhood.*

This was the divine schooling that gave rise to such a profound admiration, respect and reverence for holy scripture. This was the teaching by which David and his seed were inspired, imbrued, filled with the words of God. This was the substance and matter of all the prophecy which followed.

In amazement the great doctors of the schools of the rabbis cried, 'How knoweth this man letters, having never learned?' And saith David in spirit, 'I have more understanding than all my teachers. I understand more than the ancients.'

Yet over and above the study and understanding of all learning, in which David excelled; clear above, and transcending all knowledge, stood the prophetic gift, the seer's vision, the divine revelation. For here was pure heavenly inspiration that lifted everything beyond the reach of man.

The hand and training of professional teachers in religious or natural knowledge, never was laid upon David. Nor upon his seed. Man had nothing whatever to do with the education of either. No school, academy, college or university had anything at all to do with the development of either David or his seed; no, nor their talents, abilities, mind, character or personality.

No, because God did that, and God alone. God did it, godliness achieved it, and humility received it. The lonely sheepfold, the solitary hills, the wild mountain tops, the night seasons, the praying vigils, the long silent hours in the closet: these witnessed the teaching of God.

No eye beheld it. There is a path which no fowl knoweth, and which the vulture's eye hath not seen. This is the way of highest elevation.

This was the secret of the Lord, this preparation of the man, and it is with them that fear him. Thus was developed the prophet of the Lord, and thus is developed the manhood that goes with it. Not otherwise shall it appear.

And here is a divine principle that is just about universally unrecognised. It has been neglected, derided and despised by comparatively recent generations and certainly is by the present one. That is why they cannot understand David. Nor his seed. 'How can ye believe, which receive honour one of another?'

But David honoured God, and God honoured David, and put his words into his mouth. He learned the lessons of the school of God; he waited long years under heart-breaking and humiliating providences, till God himself wrought the change.

O, David was a man. What a man he was. He learned in heart-broken and humble submission under the chastening dealings and spiritual teachings of the Almighty. That made the prophet. That was what produced God's prophet.

The work of man, the teaching of man, the honour of man, all that man can do, recognise or bestow, had neither part nor lot in the matter.

But now it is the day of man, of human organisation, of the world's achievement. Human activity dominates the day. It is the day of man's self-development. Now, man makes the man.

The solitary place, the stillness, the desert, the wilderness, the arabia, needed to foster the prophet of God, have all been despised in favour of the city. Thus the sight and the gift have well nigh vanished from our generation.

For it was God that developed David's manhood, ability, and talent. He was the author and originator of all David's maturity, ministry, and utterance. In particular, of the divine matter as well as the heavenly vision of his prophecies, 'As the Holy Ghost spake by the mouth of David.'

Now then, this is the way that David prefigured the truth — in origin, vision and content — of the fact and the manner in which God raised up in the house of his servant David the ultimate and absolute prophet. And therefore, God's prophetic king.

This is Abraham's seed, the root and offspring of David, Jesus Christ, the Messiah, the Son of God:

'This is my beloved Son: hear him.'

Now then, in the second place,

- **David was a priestly king.**

This is the next thing which distinguished David's reign. It was of the essence to his royalty. A rare quality; it was a most distinctive feature in the king. David's royalty was priestly. David was a priestly king.

David wore the ephod, that two-sided garment which marked out before Jehovah on the one hand, and Israel on the other, that mediator between God and man. This mediator must appear with a suited sacrifice, able to propitiate the one and reconcile the other in one body.

A priest. God's priest. The royal priest. 'A priest for ever after the order of Melchizedek.' So spake King David in the great prophetic utterance of the one hundred and tenth psalm. This declared the priestly order of the coming mediator, able to reach to God in his nature, and man in his humanity.

This is the psalm quoted by Christ himself, using the opening words when proving his own deity to the consternation of the Pharisees.

> 'The LORD said unto my Lord,
> Sit thou at my right hand,
> until I make thine enemies
> thy footstool.'

**And again,**

> 'The LORD shall send the rod of thy strength
> out of Zion.'

Once more,

'The LORD hath sworn, and will not repent,
Thou art a priest for ever
after the order of Melchizedek.'

*Psalm 110, verses 1, 2 and 4.*

Thus prophesied David of his promised seed. David, observe, is the narrator, and he is speaking about Christ. Particularly. Particularly, that is, in relation to Christ's priestly and mediatorial office. David recognises that the true Mediator must reach to God in his nature, and man in his humanity.

But how? How can any priest do that?

No old testament Levitical priest could do it: they hardly even reached to man in his humanity, witness Nadab, Abihu, or the children of Eli, all of them sons of Aaron the priest. And as to reaching to God, Aaron and all the priesthood were prevented from doing that in the very nature of their service: they served outside the veil of the house of God. But God was within the veil. Then their priesthood could not reach to God. And save the high priest when typifying Christ once a year, it never did.

David saw this; he saw the need of another priesthood, he saw the need of a mediator of a better covenant, he recognised that God must be reached and humanity too, if priesthood were ever to prove effectual. But how?

That is what Psalm 110 prophesies. How. David narrates in the opening sentence of verse 1:

'The LORD said unto my Lord.'

## The Son of God

Here David himself did homage to the Son of God, whom he acknowledged as 'my Lord'. That is, David's Lord. David's Lord was the Son. Christ says so expressly. But,

'*The* LORD said unto my Lord.'

It is not that David said anything to his Lord. *The* Lord said something to *David's* Lord. Evidently David in spirit heard one speak to his Lord. 'The LORD said unto my Lord.'

Now, who is this that thus speaketh to the Son of God?

Well, consider what is spoken. Spoken? Rather, commanded! It is imperative: 'Sit thou at my right hand.' Now, at what time was this actually said to the Son of God, David's Lord? Over one thousand years after David wrote it! Precisely, at the ascension, as interprets no less an authority than the holy apostle Peter and at so significant a time as the day of Pentecost. Saith Peter,

'This Jesus hath God raised up,
whereof we all are witnesses.
Therefore being by the right hand of God exalted,
and having received of the Father
the promise of the Holy Ghost,
he hath shed forth this,
which ye now see and hear.
For David is not ascended into the heavens:
but he saith himself,
The LORD said unto my Lord,
Sit thou on my right hand.'

*Acts of the Apostles 2:32-34.*

126

Since it is the Son that ascended to the right hand of the Father, and it is to him that Peter expressly applies the imperative of the 110th Psalm written one thousand years before

'Sit thou at my right hand,'

it follows of necessity that this is a communication between the Father and the Son, after the cross, and on the day when Christ ascended, that is, at the conclusion of the forty days of Jesus' resurrection appearance on earth. Then it was that Jesus ascended into the heavens in answer to the command:

'Sit thou at my right hand.'

So saith the LORD to David's Lord. On the day of ascension. Evidently then it is God the Father who said these things to the Son, overheard beforehand by David in the spirit of prophecy. A thousand years beforehand. And if that foresight should seem incredible, it is by no means so incredible as the fact that what was foreseen actually took place in the event.

However, as to the expression

'The LORD said unto my Lord,'

we now gather beyond dispute that the Father said this to the Son. And the remarkable thing about this is not chiefly that David heard it one thousand years before it was commanded. It is that David heard it at all.

Because it means that David worshipped God and the Father as a distinct divine person, calling him THE LORD

— as opposed to 'my Lord' — saying, 'The LORD said unto my Lord.' That is, the Father said to the Son. So then David perceived the Father and the Son. And he did so over a thousand years before the actual introduction of the New Testament!

I may add that David was also well able to distinguish the divine person of the Holy Ghost. For one thing 'David spake by the Holy Ghost' in Psalm 110 as in all the psalms, knowing full well the one by whom he gave utterance. And for another thing, Peter says of Christ:

'Therefore being by the right hand of God exalted,
and having received of the Father
the promise of the Holy Ghost,
he hath shed forth this,
which ye now see and hear.'

By the first expression, 'Being by the right hand of God exalted,' Peter interprets the word in Psalm 110, 'Sit thou at my right hand.' That is, Christ is ascended to the right hand of the Father as David before prophesied.

But not to do nothing. Rather, from thence, David continues, Christ sends

'the rod of his strength out of Zion.'

Now this refers to the Holy Ghost being sent to the church to do his own work on earth in conjunction with the Son of God in heaven. Peter interprets that on this wise:

'Being by the right hand of God exalted,
and having received of the Father
the promise of the Holy Ghost,

*he hath shed forth this,*
*which ye now see and hear.'*

That is, the Son has shed forth from heaven what the disciples then saw and heard on earth. Namely 'the rod of his strength', the power of the Holy Ghost below. As he said, 'Ye shall receive power, after that the Holy Ghost is come upon you.' That is, the rod of Christ's strength.

The staggering thing is, David understood all this. He perceived and spoke of these things beforehand in the spirit of prophecy.

Now consider what David has revealed in no more than these two verses — even no more than the first sentence — of Psalm 110:

He has set before us the Father, the Son, and the Holy Ghost: one God. He has implied the incarnation, the Son of God come of the seed of David according to the flesh. He has shown us the divine and human natures of Christ in one person, namely, David's son and David's Lord. And he shows that person as heir to David's throne, ascended above all heavens. If so, then raised from the dead, the cross and the tomb having been taken for granted before the psalm opens.

David declares the Holy Ghost given, and his rule and administration in the saints below. Meanwhile he points to the ascended Son, declaring him mediator and priest: 'Thou art a priest,' Psalm 110:4. And not to be repented of: 'The LORD hath sworn with an oath.'

All that — without in any way stretching or forcing the text. After all, Peter in Acts is the one who has interpreted it — all that, I say, is found in no more than verses one and four with just a line from verse two added. This is not to treat of the other verses of the psalm nor the whole psalm itself.

Wonderful. 'In all the scriptures the things concerning himself.' Well, the scripture is the place where those things are to be found. Full of the knowledge of Christ. And, not least, Christ as distinctively prefigured by David. For the scriptures reveal Christ a priest and a king.

'A priest for ever after the order of Melchizedek,'

*Psalm 110:4.*

This being so, certain things follow of necessity. Such a divine statement has tremendous repercussions. For example, the entire old priestly system is rendered obsolete at a stroke. Because the priesthood to which God has now pointed in Psalm 110, the priesthood which alone can satisfy him and render him propitious, this priesthood forthwith excludes all other.

The Levitical priesthood under the old testament may have stood in for the time being as an imperfect and temporary type or figure, but it never did, never could, and never will satisfy God.

How much less then, all latter-day inventions of men imposed upon the church in tawdry imitation of that ancient Levitical shadow?

For in the priesthood of Christ the light has come which cast the shadow, and at once we see in the singular 'Thou art a priest,' that there are no others. It is not, 'You are.'

As to that new testament priesthood after the order of Melchizedek, we conclude that:

1.  It is not Levitical.
2.  Neither is it of the law.
3.  It is not of man after the flesh.
4.  Nor does it pertain to this present world.
5.  It does not have incompatible sacrifices.

### *1. Christ's priesthood is not Levitical.*

The priesthood of this royal seed which King David foreshadowed and of which he prophesied, was to come from his own house: 'Of the house of David.' The Christ was to come 'of the seed of David according to the flesh.' Then neither he nor his priesthood could be Levitical.

Obviously, Christ, the chosen, the royal priest of God, could not be of the tribe of Levi. Of necessity he must arise from the same tribe as his father David. And this important and far-reaching truth is pointed out in the epistle to the Hebrews: 'For it is evident that our Lord sprang out of Juda,' Hebrews 7:14.

Far-reaching, for immediately the verse goes on to say, 'Of which tribe Moses spake nothing concerning priesthood.' No, Moses did not, but David did. Moses did not, because he personified the old legal system of human works. David did, because he prefigured the new divine administration of free grace.

But what did David speak as concerning priesthood? He

prophesied of one who was of his own house, sprung of the tribe of Judah, that is, the Lion of the tribe of Judah, saying,

> 'Thou art a priest for ever
> after the order of Melchizedek.'

A priestly king of the royal tribe of Judah.

Of course, no one denies that Moses did speak of a tribe as concerning priesthood. Certainly he did, and that tribe was the tribe of Levi, Aaron's tribe. Moses' tribe, too, come to that. Aaron and his sons, with the Levites and the Levitical priesthood ministered about the things which Moses delivered. Legal things. Things pertaining to works required by the law. They were, in fact, ministers of the law.

But what on earth is that to do with the son of David?

To your tents, O Israel!

> 'If therefore perfection were by the Levitical priesthood,
> (for under it the people received the law,)
> what further need was there
> that another priest should rise
> after the order of Melchisedec,
> and not be called after the order of Aaron?
> For the priesthood being changed,
> there is made of necessity
> a change also of the law.'
>
> *Hebrews 7:11,12.*

### 2. Christ's priesthood is not of the law.

That is what we see in King David's priestly seed, sprung of Judah's tribe, called after the order of Melchizedek:

> 'The priesthood being changed,
> there is made of necessity
> a change also of the law.'

Wherefore those who have Christ Jesus to their priest, are not under the law. For Christ Jesus is not a minister of the law. Far from it, he is a deliverer from the law. He is a minister of grace. He is the end of the law for righteousness to every one that believeth.

Christ is the minister of grace, grace which reigns through righteousness unto eternal life by Jesus Christ our Lord. All who trust in this one mediator therefore discover to themselves that they are not under the law; no, not in any shape or form, nor in any subtle distinction; not moral, ceremonial, or judicial law:

> 'For ye are *not* under the law,
> but under grace.'

Christ reigns, a priest for ever after the order of Melchizedek, and hence indicates the end of the Levitical order and of necessity a change in the law. Instead of the law, for the believer there is Christ alone. 'They saw no man' — no, neither Moses nor Elias — 'save Jesus only.'

It is not that the law is arbitrarily cast aside as disposable. It is not that with mindless contempt the law is summarily dismissed. It is not that the law is abrogated and so made vain. God forbid! The self-righteous legalists do that; they advocate a law they can never keep. They bring the law into contempt by talking of something their lives insult and deny. They make void the law with a vengeance. Self-righteous hypocrites, they neither know what they say, nor whereof they affirm.

But Christ delivers us from the law. Not by changing it in itself, even he cannot do that; but by changing us and our position in relation to it. He makes a change in our relationship to the law by taking us out of its reach. And wherever is out of the law's reach? The other side of death!

Death satisfies the law. It can rest with that. Death meets its last demand. It has nothing to say to the dead. Well,

> 'I through the law am dead to the law:
> I am crucified with Christ.'

Out of reach. The law honoured. But the believer delivered. What a priesthood! Wonderful Lord Jesus!

So then, believers are in a changed position with regard to the law. It is not changed, but they are in a changed position in respect of it, and the cause is, that the law regards them as dead in Christ. The law is not dead, but believers are dead to it. It legislates no rule of moral obligation, it has no requirements in respect of the dead. It makes no demands from dead men.

As to its broken precepts, the same death met them as delivers from the very law itself. 'Christ hath redeemed us from the curse of the law, being made a curse for us,' on the one hand. And on the other, 'God sent forth his Son, made of a woman, made under the law, to redeem them that were under the law, that we might receive the adoption of sons.' Galatians 3:13 and 4:4,5. Redeemed by death from the broken precepts of the law and also from the law itself. The future? 'So then, ye are not under the law, but under grace.' 'For ye are dead, and your life is hid with Christ in God.'

'A change in the law' indicated by a change in the priesthood. But why was the priesthood changed?

For two reasons.

*(i)* 'For the law made nothing perfect,' Hebrews 7:19. Nothing and nobody. To the contrary, it condemned everything and everybody. All who are under it are under a curse, as it is written, 'Cursed is every one that continueth not in all things which are written in the book of the law to do them.' Cursing follows the law, and condemnation follows the curse. The law worketh wrath.

'For the law made nothing perfect, but the bringing in of a better hope did.' Did what? Did make everything perfect.

What better hope is this? That God would give to man another priesthood than he deserved. Which is what happened, saying to that singular and unique priesthood in David, 'Thou art a priest for ever after the order of Melchizedek.' That priest made everything perfect,

> 'For by one offering he hath perfected for ever them that are sanctified.'

*(ii)* The second reason for changing the priesthood was this: the Levitical priesthood was a hopeless failure both in

itself, and in its complete inability to do anything for those whom it served. And so it is for all ministry under the law, and every legal minister unto this day. In fact, such are a complete delusion. Disguising their own personal failure, they pretend to have the answer for others. They have no answer at all.

Only Christ, and Christ exclusively, has the answer. That is what it says:

> 'If therefore perfection were by the Levitical priesthood, (for under it the people received the law,)'

well, if so, then what?

> 'What further need was there
> that another priest should rise
> after the order of Melchizedek?'

None whatever. No further need whatever. None at all. If the law could possibly have given any hope to man in any shape, form, part, or particular, there would have been no need at all for Christ's priesthood. Nor his death. 'For if righteousness come by the law, then Christ is dead in vain.' Nor his life. 'No further need for another priest.'

But the rise in fact of another priest than that of the law proves demonstrably that there is neither present hope nor future prospect under the law. Otherwise, why Christ's priesthood?

Because under the law, and under ministers of the law, and under a legal ministry, nothing whatsoever can be done for the poor deluded and hopeless souls that trust in it. The only hope, the better hope, the sole prospect, is to be redeemed out from under the law, and hence delivered from the old legal ministers who, given their will, would entangle us for ever under the yoke of bondage.

But be assured, my brethren, under Christ, 'We are redeemed from the law.' The bringing in of a better hope is this: that 'ye also are become dead to the law by the body of Christ.' For 'now we are delivered from the law, that being dead wherein we were held.' And, 'I through the law am dead to the law, that I might live unto God.' 'I am crucified with Christ.'

What a proper priesthood for men!

For there is one God, and one mediator between God and men, the man Christ Jesus, made a priest for ever after the order of Melchizedek. He makes all things perfect, which is not surprising, for he is perfection personified.

But the other factor on the subject is this: Not only is it true that the Levitical priesthood could make nothing perfect, but imperfection was already within the priests before they began the work of ministering to others.

Then how could such a priesthood help others to overcome the things that overcame it? How could such a priesthood disentangle others from the things with which it itself was entangled? It could not.

How imperfect was that priesthood! Yet it was no more than typical of men right from the beginning. And since what was typical of men had caused the fall and separated mankind from God, how could what was typical bring mankind back? Right from the beginning Levi showed this inconsistency.

Who made the golden calf, when Moses was in the mount, causing Israel to sin by idolatry? It was Aaron, the father of the Levitical priesthood. With whom did Miriam — smitten with leprosy for her impudence — I say, with whom did Miriam work rebellion against the Lord and Moses in the wilderness? With Aaron, the father of the Levitical priesthood. And with whom was the anger of the Lord kindled in that great wilderness? The scripture saith, 'And the Lord was very angry with Aaron.'

Then how could perfection possibly come from that priesthood which sprang from him?

Someone may say, But that is not the whole story: you are too particular. No, not at all. I reply, You are too general. We are talking about priesthood, not the people. Those who must represent the imperfect people before God. We are talking about what God requires from such. Perfection. We are talking about perfection. 'If therefore *perfection* were by the Levitical priesthood, what further need was there for another priest?'

If our priesthood is not perfection personified, we are served by a delusion.

But before the very best priesthood that man could produce, the one chosen by God to stand in till Christ should come, the Levitical priesthood, I say, before that priesthood was even consecrated, it sinned. Then how could it act for sinners once it was consecrated? It was no better than they were, no closer to God, just as far away.

So is every human priesthood. With this difference: the Levitical priesthood *was* ordained of God for the time then present until the coming of Christ. But the invented, unconsecrated, unordained priesthoods under pope and patriarch, primate and archbishop *, these are not only just as imperfect as Levi, sharing all the Levitical disqualifications, but they have two further liabilities.

First. They have no authority from God for their existence whatsoever. The very idea of clerical priesthood in the church — mingled with 'evangelical' fellow-travellers, if you please — is a total fabrication without apostolic or scriptural authority. Both unlawful and unevangelical.

Second. The Levitical priesthood was there when Christ's priesthood was not there. But now Christ is there — the exclusive priest, the perfect priest, the sole chosen of God — now, I say, that he is there, these usurpers wilfully and deliberately defy him and his present ministry, knowingly putting themselves in his place *. Contemptible rebels; thanks be to God, the Lord shall have them in derision.

See what man's priesthood achieves! Before the seven days of consecration at the very beginning were even completed, whilst the oil of anointing was fresh upon them, the sons of Aaron carelessly disobeyed the Lord in their imperfection, offering strange fire before the Lord which he commanded them not.

It doesn't matter *that* much, this imperfection? 'And there went out fire from the Lord, and devoured them, and they died before the Lord.' If imperfection did not matter, they had not died, and Christ would not have come.

* See 'The Gospel of God', Tract for the Times No. 1. The Publishing Trust. Price 25p.

139

How could any priesthood that is of man, that depends upon man — even given the authority of having been chosen of God as a type — how *could* it make the comers thereunto perfect? It could not. It is impossible.

But perfection God will have, and must have, else none shall come near his presence, neither for time nor eternity. But perfection is precisely what Christ brings in, and only he can bring in, and that is why he came: to make the comers thereunto perfect. Perfect. Christ makes perfect. The law, men, and human priesthood cannot. Never could and never will.

Now I pass on to the third point about Christ's royal priesthood after the order of Melchizedek:

*3. Christ's priesthood is not of man after the flesh.*

Besides all that has been said, there is this to be added: The Levitical priesthood was after the flesh. 'Made after the law of a carnal' — fleshly — 'commandment.' That is, it was of the flesh; just as all that is of man is after the flesh.

One asks, What does this mean, 'After the flesh'? Well, what happens to the flesh? It cannot be preserved, it ages, it corrupts, it dies, it rots.

And how can that please God? It cannot. Such mortality is highly displeasing to the very nature of the Eternal. A constant reminder of the ageing, rotting, dying nature of the priesthood which he permitted as a type for the time being, till Christ should come.

'They truly were many priests,
because they were not suffered to continue
by reason of death.'

*Hebrews 7:23.*

Reason of death? But what is the cause of death? 'Death passed upon all men, for that all have sinned.' Sin is the cause of death. Indeed, 'The wages of sin is death.' But the Levitical priesthood died, just the same — and for the same cause — as those whom it purported to represent before the living God.

'By reason of death.' So they died because of sin. Just as those whom they served died because of sin. Then how can such sinners plead in behalf of the sinful? And who is to plead for them? For evidently they need a priest, as much as those whose priesthood they are! Carnal themselves, needing to offer sacrifices first for themselves, then for the people; and after all their sacrifices, still perishing in their turn: who shall plead for these dying sons of Aaron?

Why, him of whom they were the temporary types and figures. The very one of whom they were the shadow. The one mediator, the man Christ Jesus. For if

'They truly were many priests,
because they were not suffered to continue
by reason of death:
This man,
because he continueth ever,
hath an unchangeable priesthood.'

*Hebrews 7:23,24.*

141

Well, of course. He is

'A priest *for ever* after the order of Melchizedek.'

And all this — as regards the Levitical priesthood — is not to mention the objectionableness of the flesh to God, even during the brief span in which mortals do live. 'For they that are after the flesh do mind the things of the flesh.' And again, 'To be carnally minded is death.' Once more, 'The carnal mind is enmity against God: for it is not subject to the law of God, neither indeed can be. So then they that are in the flesh cannot please God.' No wonder the conclusion of the matter is this: 'Flesh and blood cannot inherit the kingdom of God.'

What a tremendous need then, for those Levitical priests to look for a priest to come, who should dispense at once with their collapsing era, and act henceforth for ever on their behalf, as well as for the people.

Then what a relief to them that, 'Thou art a priest for ever.'

And what vicious, horrible insolence, now that Christ has come, for the fallen and apostate church to invent — and so reintroduce — a priesthood modelled after the old order. And forthwith to invest it with the very same provocations for which God did away for ever with the obsolete old testament system. And what adding of insult to injury for 'evangelicals' to step into these hired offices for reward, meanwhile donning the forbidden robes of apostate sacramentalism.

And not content with this, now the incumbent of the ancient antichristian throne resident at the Vatican, reviving the subtle schemes of his predecessors, labours with willing allies to join all the impostorous priesthoods into one under his triple crown, cunningly devising together to unite the church under their damnable heresies.

Since Christ came, there is but one priest. Not seen with the eye, he is set forth by preaching, and his services obtained through believing. He cannot die: he has died once for all, and he is risen again world without end. Now, he is a priest for evermore.

> 'This man, because he continueth ever,
> hath an unchangeable priesthood.'

*Hebrews 7:24.*

Moreover he is made a priest by the irrevocable oath of God. This can never be retracted. 'The LORD hath sworn, and will not repent,' says David, 'Thou art a priest for ever.' The LORD sware by himself to uphold the royal priesthood of Christ for evermore. He will never take it back: not now that he has sworn it.

> 'By so much'
> — so very much —
> 'was Jesus made a surety
> of a better testament.'

Aaron and the Levitical priests had no such oath. For the simple reason that their priesthood was to be retracted. There was no thought in God's mind that it should be permanent. Hence,

> 'Those priests were made without an oath;
> but this with an oath

143

by him that said unto him,
The Lord sware and will not repent,
Thou art a priest for ever
after the order of Melchisedec.'

*Hebrews 7:21.*

As soon as Christ ascended and began the exercise of his perpetual priesthood, then the Levitical priesthood ceased to have any significance whatsoever. How could it have? Its sole purpose was to stand in till Christ came, so as to depict and typify — as best as may be — the principles of priesthood.

Once Christ came, it was finished. Done away for ever. Christ alone enshrines every priestly principle. Principles which the Levites merely depicted but could not embody. But Christ embodies all, retains every principle, and is the sole priest of God presented to mankind for faith world without end,

'Who is made,
not after the law of a carnal commandment,
but after the power of an endless life.'

'This man,
because he continueth ever,
hath an unchangeable priesthood.'

God will not, God cannot reintroduce that, the failure of which was the cause of Christ's coming! And God cannot, God will not hold guiltless these antichrists who have invented their own arbitrary substitute for the abolished old testament priesthood — copying even their dress and outward show — and who have imposed the

144

result on the church in place of the glory of Christ. Let the people beware. The Lord shall surely smite both Roman, Eastern, and Anglican priesthoods with the rod of his mouth. He shall have them in derision. Then be more than careful to honour the Son alone, lest thou be partaker of both their sins and their judgment.

Christ alone is your priest!

This the apostles clearly teach you, David depicts for you, and Melchizedek typifies for all who would seek a favourable approach to God thereafter.

Melchizedek. This mysterious figure appearing in the record of Genesis 14, suddenly manifesting himself to Abraham after the slaughter of the kings. There is no doubt at all, Melchizedek depicts Christ.

How strangely Melchizedek appears in Moses' narrative. The record is written so that we know nothing that went before the appearance and are told of nothing that happened afterwards. Indeed, even the mention of the name Melchizedek was not to occur again until written by King David in Psalm 110, thousands of years after the Genesis record.

Melchizedek. A name formed by combining the Hebrew word for King, *melek*, and that for Righteousness, *tzedeq*, so making *melektzedeq;* and by a process of elision and transliteration: Melchizedek. It means by interpretation, King of righteousness. This is not his title, remark, it is his actual name. His title is King of Salem. His name, King of righteousness. Since this name is descriptive, in such a person it must be indicative of his nature.

King of righteousness; this teaches the realm of his dominion — reigning in respect of the quality of righteousness — and if so, we may say that there is no area of righteousness in which he does not personally triumph. And if as a king, then triumph on behalf of his subject people.

It is not simply that he rules in respect of the righteousness of the law. In fact the law had not been given. The king of righteousness however, rules in respect of the *quality* of righteousness. He is king of it, itself. Whether righteousness of men, or of God. Whether divine or human. Whether finite, righteousness of the creature; or infinite, righteousness of the Creator.

The quality as such is that over which the king rules. Then, above all, over the righteousness of God, because that is the ultimate in righteousness. And who has dominion there in respect of his people? Why, Messiah. Messiah

'finishes the transgression,
makes an end of sins,
makes reconciliation for iniquity,
and brings in *everlasting* righteousness,'

*Daniel 9:24.*

and he does it by the blood of his cross.

'But now the righteousness of God
without the law
is manifested,
Even the righteousness of God
which is by faith of Jesus Christ,
unto all and upon all them that believe.'

146

'That grace might reign through righteousness
unto eternal life by Jesus Christ our Lord.'

*Romans 3 and 5.*

That is it. Through dying on behalf of his people as their substitute, Christ answered all the righteous demands of the law upon unrighteous men; but far beyond anything the law could demand, the blood shed on Calvary reached right to the uttermost to satisfy every requirement of the righteousness of God in his own nature.

That is why Paul, speaking of the gospel, declares,

'Therein is the righteousness of God revealed.'

*Romans 1:17.*

Hence Melchizedek — king of righteousness — depicted Christ in the gospel by the name through which he was known. *Melek*, King. *Tsedeq*, Righteousness. Melchizedek.

Also, he is designated by the title, King of Salem. Now, Salem is Peace. Melchizedek is therefore by interpretation — or rather, translation — King of peace. Shalom.

But first king of righteousness. The basis of peace, and reigning peace, and the peace of God reigning in the heart, the basis I say, is satisfied righteousness. If the law can find no fault with us, our conscience is at peace, and the legal case rests. But if God can find no fault with us, not judging us as men according to the behaviour we should render to the law, but according to what he is in himself, according to the divine righteousness of his own nature, according to what passes between divine persons, what peace is this? Peace that passeth all understanding.

147

But how shall men, who cannot make peace with the law of God, find peace with the nature of righteousness within the Godhead?

By blood. By the blood of Jesus. By faith in his blood. That satisfied every demand, and

> 'Being justified' — reckoned righteous — 'by faith,
> we have peace with God
> through our Lord Jesus Christ.'
>
> *Romans 5:1.*

He reigns in fulfilment of all, but all righteousness, and he does so on behalf of his subject people through the sacrifice made at Calvary's cross. Then if so, he reigns in peace on their behalf, meanwhile showing them his hands and his feet, saying,

> 'Peace be unto you.'

With this, we may sit at rest, taking our meat with gladness and singleness of heart. Here is the bread and wine of plenitude. Here is that table fitly spread, speaking of and having in memorial a sacrifice complete. Here is Messiah's priestly blessing. King of righteousness. King of peace. A royal priest. A priest on the throne. Which is precisely what David foreshadowed. And what Melchizedek depicted:

> 'And Melchizedek king of Salem
> brought forth bread and wine:
> and he was the priest
> of the most high God.'
>
> *Genesis 14:18.*

He appears in the narrative without warning. He disappears without trace. He is. In a graphical figure,

> 'Without father,
> without mother,
> without descent,
> having neither beginning of days,
> nor end of life;
> but made like unto the Son of God;
> abideth a priest continually.'
>
> *Hebrews 7:3.*

Made like to the Son of God. That is, the circumstances that designed his life to be figurative of the Son, make him like that. And the way Moses narrates the record by the Holy Ghost, makes him like that. So that, the figure of the Son of God, is what the enlightened will see in the form of Melchizedek: A priest on the throne. A royal priest. The son of David.

No wonder Abraham, and in him Isaac, Jacob, and all the children of Israel — and of course all the sons of Aaron and tribe of Levi — did homage and obeisance, paying tithes to this royal priest as their superior.

And why not?

> 'For this man,
> because he continueth ever,
> hath an unchangeable priesthood.'

Not the Levites. They died. Generations of them died one after the other. And yet it is not before but after death that a priest is really needed. It is at the judgment that one

149

needs a priest to plead one's cause, standing on the right hand of Almighty God on one's behalf.

> 'For it is appointed unto men once to die,
> but after this
> the judgment.'
>
> *Hebrews 9:27.*

The Son of God, son of David, raised from the dead, possesses precisely the qualifications needed. No one else does, or could ever do so. No one other than he deserves to act as our priest.

For us to turn from him to carnal priesthoods, especially to those fabricated by decadent christendom, is to refuse the offices of the son of David, to spurn his services, to insult his nature.

Raised from the dead, he abideth a priest continually. Because of this he is able to save to the uttermost — not just for this life: for that which is to come, the uttermost — them that come unto God by him.

> 'For the law made men high priests
> which had infirmity.'

Some infirmity! He is speaking of death. They died. How then could they help after death, at the judgment? Then, they suffered the same dilemma, were in the self-same predicament, as those whom they had served in this life.

Nevertheless, at least — as types — the *law* made them high priests. But the church has absolutely no authority to make any priests at all. The very character of the church stands in this: that Christ is the exclusive priest of the faithful. And that he is received by faith alone. Then any professing body, any professing archbishop, or pontiff, or prelate, that pretends to make priests in the name of the church is nothing but a usurper of Christ. And therefore a damnable liar. An utter impostor. Which is what we have always been taught, and quite rightly so. This fashionable treachery, wet behind the ears and still in nappies, lies when it pretends to antiquity. Just as it lies in everything else.

Even the old testament priesthood, which was tolerated till Christ came, God found fault with. For, finding fault with them, he saith,

> 'The law maketh men high priests
> which have infirmity.'

However, in complete contrast with this whole idea of human priesthood, the entire conception that men might be priests, the complete system tried out under the law, I say, in utter contrast we find the following established by God himself for time and eternity to the exclusion of everything else:

> 'but the word of the oath,'

— that is, the oath declared by King David in Psalm 110, 'The LORD hath sworn, and will not repent, Thou art a priest for ever after the order of Melchizedek' —

> 'but the word of the oath,
> which was since the law,
> maketh the Son,
> *who is consecrated for evermore.'*

And if for evermore, death hath no more dominion over

him. What priest, either of those legitimate, or these illegitimate, can ever claim that?

Only Christ can say that. There can be no other. All others are nothing but bastards. It is the Son who is consecrated, from henceforth and for evermore, for life and death, for this world and that to come, for all the church in every generation: he, this royal priest, this son of David, he is the exclusive priest to all his true people, to all the faithful church. Amen.

And besides all this, there are yet many other considerations regarding Christ's royal priesthood. For example,

### 4. *Christ's priesthood is not of this world.*

The Levites, fleshly, dying, made after the law of a carnal commandment, ministered the law where the law was given: on earth. It was in this world, and God gave it for this world, and this present life was the realm of the law's jurisdiction.

To rend the law piecemeal and arbitrarily to separate the 'ten commandments' — as the scribes choose to call them — shows a lamentable ignorance of the essential idea of law.

But then to add insult to injury, and capriciously to characterise the section which they have illegally broken off as 'the moral law' — an expression of which scripture knows absolutely nothing, any more than do the legalists who 'desiring to be teachers of the law, understand neither what they say, nor whereof they affirm,' I Timothy 1:7 — this is not merely lamentable ignorance, it is dangerous folly, it is both opening the door and paving the way right back to the Galatian error.

But finally these ignorant mutilators of the law manage to trump their succession of confusing blunders with the overwhelming *faux pas* of their last great achievement. Well, this is just breathtaking.

And these are the men who have led christendom? Small wonder the church has fared no better than old-testament Israel, both histories being commensurate tales of largely apostate institutional leadership.

But to return to the blunders of the legalists. Their crowning achievement. Finally they say of their self-designated 'moral law' that it is 'the eternal law'. And that really puts out the light. That really renders confusion worse confounded. It completely overturns the cross, and undoes the deliverance which Christ wrought for us when he delivered us from the law for ever by his sacrifice.

Because if it is eternal, how can you ever escape from it? You cannot. There is no deliverance whatsoever. It will condemn you all over again, over again, over again. And after death, in eternity — since it is eternal — it will condemn you all over again, over again, over again.

From whence do these men get their wild fancies? Not from the scripture. Look and see. There is *nothing* in the scripture to support their dangerous and foolish conceits. Nothing which sanctions this confounding of law and confusion of the result with the gospel. Nothing to support their legalistic philosophies. Nothing in the scripture at all. But they seem to be pillars? What of that? God accepteth no man's person, much less any assembly's confession.

Then whence comes their doctrine? From their pride of human learning. From their love to be called 'Doctor, Doctor,' 'Reverend, Reverend.' From their haughty disdain of the simplicity of faith. From their arrogant contempt of the unlearned. From their high degrees, their pride of intellect, their scholastic achievements, their westminstarian place-seeking.

This attitude has put out the light of pure and simple revelation which requires no more than child-like trust. Self-emptied innocence. A guileless openness to the Spirit of the Lord. And the Bible. Just the Bible. Not that the true servants of the Lord have not read and read widely. They have: but with discrimination; and, more often than not, but once and then put away. And never, never, never to take the sole, exclusive and permanent place of personal revelation by the Spirit and from the word itself. The very opposite to the scribe and the Pharisee.

Now then the word is this: The law came by Moses and was ordained of angels, being recorded in the book of the law read in the ears of all the people. God testified that he had given this law by angels to Moses, and that he had begun to speak it on earth — whose voice then shook the earth; and which voice they that heard entreated that the word should not be spoken to them any more — leaving the remainder to be spoken by his servant Moses. The whole, I say, recorded in the book of the law.

With this witness. That which God began to speak had been engraved on tables of stone, originally hewn of God and afterwards by Moses. The tables were laid up within the tabernacle, a witness that although the people could not endure to the end the hearing of the voice, still, *God* had spoken it. It was his law for the people on earth even if the remainder was heard by them only through the mediatorial voice of Moses. The tables were a memorial of this truth.

Now these tables of stone, called the tables of the covenant, were kept in the ark, laid up in the holy place before the Lord, within the tabernacle. This tabernacle was made by hands, as was all its furniture, and the tables of stone withal. Although originally the work of God and the engraving of God, the first tables had been broken. The hand of Moses hewed the second, only the Lord engraved them. All else was made by man's hand.

The tabernacle itself was pegged to the earth, which was its destiny. However,

> 'Heaven is my throne,
> and earth my footstool:
> what house will ye build me?'

Yea, saith the scripture,

> 'The heaven of heavens cannot contain him.'

So then, how could a small tabernacle of a few cubits' dimension? Or how could such divine Majesty as reached above all heavens be conveyed by a few dying men ministering about their law walking backwards and forwards and to and fro this tent which their hands had made on earth?

And not so forwards. For,

> 'There was a tabernacle made, the first;
> and after the second veil,

the tabernacle which is called
the Holiest of all.'

*Hebrews 9:2,3.*

But the priests went only into the first. What signified was the second, beyond the veil, that had the ark of the covenant, the tables of stone, the mercy seat with the cherubim of glory, and the sign of the presence of the Lord. But the priests were not allowed past the veil into this second tabernacle.

So, even on earth, even with the law, even with the bare figures and shadows, even in the tabernacle made with hands, the priests going backwards and forwards between God and the people went not so far forwards. Not forwards to God at all.

However, into the second tabernacle, called the holy of holies, beyond the veil, went the high priest alone but once a year, and not without blood, which he offered for himself and for the errors of the people.

But the first principle of priesthood is that the man who needs an offering, needs a holy and spotless priest to make it on his behalf. He himself cannot come near, he is unholy. But the priest can go near, he is holy. So then, what is this, the high priest *offering for himself?* He cannot. Not if he needs an offering. If he needs that, he is unholy. Then he is the one who needs a priest! Therefore, this must be a type or figure.

And this his clothing indicated. For, laying aside the glory of his beauteous high priestly and Aaronic garments, on this one day, this day of days, this day of atonement,

Yom Kippur, he must not appear within the veil in his own official dress. He is required to lay aside the glorious high priestly garments in which he ministers habitually outside the veil in his proper service to Israel.

He must put off his high priestly robes, those ornate and resplendent vestments in which he showed the outward form, glory, pomp and ceremony of the old exterior and typical priestly order. He must lay them aside, I say, thereby depicting that another priesthood was to come, of which he would now act as the figure on the day of atonement.

Washing his flesh and changing his clothes completely, he dressed in garments utterly different from his own. This signified that other, that coming, that better priesthood of which he was now to be the figure.

The high priest now clothed himself all in pure linen, head to foot, all in white, a spotless figure, as it were shining in the radiant glory and inward purity of the one true mediator between God and men, the coming Messiah. All in white, all outward show and worldly glory despised, the high priest depicts the one of whom he was but the poor earthly shadow, in but a poor and worldly tabernacle.

> 'The Holy Ghost this signifying,
> that the way into the Holiest of all
> was not yet made manifest,
> while as the first tabernacle was yet standing.'

It was a figure for the time then present, signified by the tabernacle made with hands, in the age that now exists, on the earth as now standing, with the law speaking in this present world: a figure. A pattern. A pattern of the heavenly, a picture of the tabernacle high in the heavens, not made with hands, eternal, everlasting, one far above this world and the law in it, one that resounds with nothing but grace, free grace, world without end. Amen.

Now that Christ has come of the seed of David according to the flesh — that royal, priestly seed of promise — having been crucified, buried, and raised from the dead, he is made higher than the heavens.

He has taken away every veil and rent them for ever asunder. He has superseded every priesthood and rendered all that man can do obsolete for ever. He has fulfilled every type and shadow, and made redundant the poor patterns of heavenly things which once served as tabernacles and temples here below. He has delivered the faithful out of this world and the law that speaks to men whilst alive in it, raising them by his own life and power into that heavenly and everlasting realm where grace alone reigns through righteousness unto eternal life by Jesus Christ our Lord.

> 'Sat down on the right hand
> of the throne of the Majesty
> in the heavens:
> A minister of the sanctuary,
> and of the true tabernacle,
> which the Lord pitched,
> and not man.'

For Christ is not entered into the holy places made with hands, which are figures of the true. Christ is not in the realm where the law speaks on earth, legislates in the world, judges in this present life.

He has ascended far above all; above all that is temporal,

far above all the earth and the sky, far above death, far beyond the grave, far past where the law was spoken and still speaks, far over this present age, far above,

'into heaven itself,
now to appear in the presence of God
for us.'

Which thing the tribe of Levi and sons of Aaron could never do. They were made priests after the law, carnal and dying, imperfect and fraught with infirmity, ministering in what men made with hands — even then after a pattern — chained to the earth, doomed to the grave, destined for the tomb. They were imprisoned in this world, trapped beneath the law, condemned under the curse.

But Christ has ascended far over all. And this is a thing Levi and the sons of Aaron could never do. They could never, no, never, never, never, ascend into heaven itself, never appear in the presence of God for us.

Yet that is what a priest must do in order effectually to qualify for the title priest. Before, under the old covenant, God suffered the types. Now, the singular priesthood of Christ is confirmed with an oath for evermore.

For Christ, having done this, and now being ascended, he has dispensed for ever with the need for any priesthood other than his, world without end. Amen.

Thus the royal priest, the priest for ever, the priest and king. So different from the priesthood of men, for

*5. Christ's priesthood does not have incompatible sacrifices.*

The sons of Aaron, the priests, offered sacrifices for sinners. Why? Evidently because sinners need sacrifices to satisfy the broken law and propitiate an offended God. And sacrifices cannot be offered by the sinful. A holy priesthood acceptable to God, must mediate and make the offering.

Well and good; but what is this, that the sons of Aaron offered first for themselves? If they required sacrifices, then they were sinners. And if they were sinners, how could they be a holy priesthood acceptable to God as mediators on behalf of others? Come to that, how could they offer for themselves? If they needed a sacrifice, then they were not holy enough to make the offering. Then who and where was their priest?

At best how imperfect the types. That the old testament figure of priesthood breaks down, reveals yet another way in which the Spirit points us to the absolute necessity for the one true reality: Christ, the son of David, the priest for ever after the order of Melchizedek.

And what about the sacrifices themselves, which were offered under the law? Consider.

For whom were these sacrifices made? For Israel. For those, and those exclusively, to whom the law was given. For immortal souls under covenant to Jehovah. For the children of Israel who, if fallen, were accountable human beings created in the image of God. Rational, responsible Israel, under obligation to God's holy law, and answerable for obedience to the intent, the quality, and the content of that law.

This had nothing to do with the Gentiles; and they, without God in the world, outside the commonwealth of Israel, had nothing to do with it. Nor the covenant.

The children of Israel were the persons for whom the sacrifices were instituted and offered by the priesthood. Instituted, because with the giving of the obligatory law on Sinai was the recognition that it would be perpetually broken by responsible Israel, accountable to God for obedience. Or disobedience. The sacrifices were for the disobedient. Except where the disobedience was too outrageous. Then, there was nothing but the judgment.

That is how it was in fact. Although the sheer confusion I have met with on this and correlated subjects by the people who are supposed to teach us is nobody's business. I do not think I will ever get over the sense of outrage — after I had been called of the Lord and sought his truth — when first I discovered the astounding ignorance that lay behind such supercilious condescension on the part of the clergy, their traditions, their traditional teaching, and their traditional teachers. Talk about blind leaders of the blind.

First then, the children of Israel, under law, were the ones for whom the sacrifices were made. They were offered by the chosen Levitical priesthood, and they were made to render satisfaction for the disobedient Israelites when they had transgressed the law. Unless the transgression was too iniquitous to warrant sacrifice. Then they died without mercy under two or three witnesses.

Now, what were these sacrifices offered by the elect priesthood on behalf of accountable but disobedient Israel?

Animals. They offered animals from the herd and the flock together with certain selected birds. Oxen were offered, bulls, cows, calves; sheep were sacrificed, rams, ewes, and lambs; goats, he goats and she goats with their kids. Besides this turtledoves, young pigeons, and small birds, sparrows.

These were offered as an atonement — cover, really — in place of the punishment due to the person for whom the offering was being made. Substitutes they were. It was substitutionary atonement. The law was satisfied. The judge exonerated in showing mercy. And the sinner was freed with a good conscience, the price having been paid. That was, and still is, the principle of sacrifice.

But animals?

What sort of substitutes were these? In place of persons? Animal sacrifices, dead animals, brute beasts of the field? Standing in as substitutes for rational human beings, under the highest of obligations, accountable to Jehovah, the most high God? Animals? Impossible.

Impossible, because the two things are not compatible. Such beasts are in no way commensurate with those persons for whom they were offered. Therefore neither can their suffering or death count in the eyes of the law, or the judge, as being equal to that due from condemned men.

In fact these beasts of the field bear about as much relationship to men, as the fowls of the air do to angels. They are not compatible. They are absurdly disparate.

Therefore animals cannot possibly be acceptable to the law in the place of accountable human beings. They cannot pay the account for the simple reason that they are dumb brutes, without obligation or morality. And if they cannot answer to man, then certainly they cannot pay his account. They are not equivalent. They cannot stand in the place of men. They are so much lower an order of life as to be ruled completely out of court.

But it was animal sacrifices that constituted the service of the legal priesthood. And on which the legal system rested. Yet we have seen that any comparison with or substitution for men is not just unequal: it is illegal!

Here is but one more example of the total inadequacy of the figures and shadows of the old testament and legal system. And one the fallacy of which the offerers were intended to understand. So that they might look through the shadows — meanwhile learning the elemental principles which they conveyed — look through them, to the light of a priesthood yet to come, which should fulfil all things.

Just as to us, so to the seeking Israelite, it must have been obvious that the sacrifices could have been no more than types, and most inadequate types at that. Nevertheless, showing to the offerer certain basic conceptions:

□ That substitutionary atonement is absolutely essential to acceptance with God. One must have a slain sacrifice in order to appear in the divine presence.

□ That God's chosen priesthood must present that sacrifice on one's behalf. The priest must come from God to the offerer; he must make the sacrifice; and it is he that must take the blood of that sacrifice back to God. The offerer cannot take one step nearer to the house of God than the altar. All else is priestly ground.

□ That a divinely chosen, lawfully slain sacrifice must stand in, instead of oneself, to bear away sin incurred through breaking the law of God. The blood of this sacrifice must be taken in and received acceptably in the presence of God, in order for the guilty offerer to know that he is forgiven. The priest, on his reappearance from within the holy place, must give this assurance in person.

□ That sin is ingrained, inbred, and will outwork. That the law condemns sin. That it is deadly serious. That there must be death to silence the law. But that adequate sacrifice is provided save for certain heinous sins which are unforgivable. That there must be blood to appease the wrath of God. For without the shedding of blood is no remission of sin.

Now, the Levitical priesthood and sacrifices undoubtedly taught these things, and taught them as clearly as types and figures could possibly do so. But the two things used for this teaching — human priesthood and animal sacrifices — showed that they were patently inadequate in themselves to answer to what they taught.

For true fulfilment, as both types and prophecy

emphasised, one was to look to the coming Messiah, a priest for ever after the order of Melchizedek.

Until then one must regard the coming One by faith through the transient figures of Levitical priesthood and animal sacrifice. At least that showed beyond any doubt just how seriously sin is to be regarded. However, such sacrifices were as obviously unacceptable to a just and holy God, as they were incompatible to reasonable and intelligent men.

Unequal to the task of substitution; inadequate for the place of atonement; not commensurate with what was demanded in retribution by the law; incompatible in every way possible. What appeared to the understanding was this:

'For it is not possible
that the blood of bulls and of goats
should take away sins.'

'In burnt offerings and sacrifices for sin
thou hast had no pleasure.'

*Hebrews 10:4 and 6.*

No pleasure, no, and for precisely the reason given: beasts of the field simply were not acceptable as substitutes for men made in the image of God. Therefore their death could not be put to the account of men. Nor could their blood signify as having vicariously paid the price of human sin.

It could not, and it did not. What it did was to signify a sacrifice to come which would be the equivalent to men. A sacrifice whose blood put to their account would pay the debt of sinners and absolve them from all charges, justifying them completely by blood accepted vicariously.

The name of the one yielding this vicarious sacrifice is JESUS, for

'He shall save his people from their sins.'

*Matthew 1:21.*

'This man,
after he had offered one sacrifice for sins for ever,
sat down on the right hand of God.'

*Hebrews 10:12.*

So you may see, this priest for ever after the order of Melchizedek, this royal priest, whom David typified and of whom he prophesied, Christ Jesus, is in contrast to all that went before. Even though there was much that inadequately typified him, still, for all that, he was clearly set forth as in contrast to the entire legal system.

- □ His priesthood was not Levitical.

- □ It was not without an oath.

- □ It was nothing to do with the law.

- □ Nor was it after the flesh.

- □ Neither did it pertain to this present world.

- □ Nor was his sacrifice incompatible.

To the contrary, unlike the Levites:

- His priesthood is royal, of the seed of David, and after the order of Melchizedek.

- His priesthood is sworn by the irrevocable oath of God, and can never be retracted.

- His priesthood delivers from the law, refuses works, speaks to faith and is on the basis of grace.

- His priesthood is since the resurrection, exercised in heaven, is from the glory, and stands in the power of an endless life.

- His priesthood justifies for, gives title to, and establishes within the world to come unto everlasting ages.

- His sacrifice perfects for ever them that are sanctified, and his blood cleanses from all sin, justifying not only from the law of Moses, but reaches so far as unto the very righteousness of God himself.

Such a priest with so satisfactory a sacrifice, may truly be described as royal. A royal priest, and a priestly king. This, David prefigured.

Moreover King David, of whose seed came the royal priest, drew attention by the Spirit to what had been shrouded in darkness for thousands of years: the strange narrative of Moses concerning Melchizedek, king of Salem.

David saw this hidden meaning. He applied it to Christ in his prophecy. And he did so by adding to the revealed mystery the extraordinary divine utterance to which his ears were opened. He heard the oath of God. He heard the Father sware to the Son as concerning his priesthood. David understood the royal priesthood.

He took up his pen and wrote in prophecy what he had heard from heaven spoken of his royal seed, spoken to the Son of God:

'The LORD hath sworn, and will not repent,
Thou art a priest for ever
after the order of Melchizedek.'

This leads me to the third and last observation:

- **David was an absolute king.**

He did not become king by popular majority. He was ordained king by divine election. His was not a 'constitutional monarchy' — all constitution and no monarchy — stripped of real power save to endorse the decisions of the actual government.

David's rule was autocratic; his power unlimited in the kingdom: he himself made the decisions. His was the government. It was upon his shoulder.

His monarchy was absolute; he was answerable to none but Jehovah. It was God that had established David's throne. The crowning of David was the initiative of the Most High. The Lord of hosts had commanded his anointing. David's throne was established through divine prerogative; man had nothing to do with it. Jehovah's decree to the people was this:

> 'Yet have I set my king
> upon my holy hill of Zion.'

*Psalm 2:6.*

This was not because of the will of the people. It was because of the will of God. In the case of the second psalm it was despite the will of the people. It is, 'Yet have *I* set *my* king.' It is for the people to submit. But to this men are not inclined.

God foretells and forewarns that the king shall inherit, rule, and judge the whole earth at the time appointed.

Then what shall be the lot of the two-faced hypocrite in Zion? Then what of the double-minded profession of Christianity, grown greater — as a great mustard tree — than the poor and despised reality? And what of the rebellious, the disobedient; in a word, the heathen?

Saith God to his king, The heathen? Ask of me, and I shall give thee the heathen for thine inheritance, and the uttermost parts of the earth for thy possession. The heathen?

> 'Thou shalt break them
> with a rod of iron;
> thou shalt dash them in pieces
> like a potter's vessel.'

## The Son of God

In view of this the world rulers are counselled,

'Be wise now therefore,
O ye kings:
be instructed,
ye judges of the earth.'

*Psalm 2:8-10.*

This prophecy of David makes it abundantly clear — and his own rule clearly depicts — that God's king is an absolute monarch. And not just over Israel. His title is King of kings, and he is destined for world dominion.

It is the last thing that appears at present. But it shall surely come to pass at his appearing and his kingdom. The purpose, will, election, predestination, promise, oath, and providence of God are set upon it.

The same determinate counsel and foreknowledge of God that sent his Son into the world, achieving every objective intended before he left it, is that which also has pledged his coming kingdom. What could be more certain? What is promised, as yet to come, is no more difficult to achieve than what has already been accomplished. Since the latter has passed into history, the future is therefore certainly assured.

God has absolutely committed himself, taken himself to oath; he has publicly pledged his determination to see every promise to Christ fulfilled, especially that of the coming kingdom. He shall inherit the earth and reign, and of his kingdom and dominion there shall be no end. And all this is not so far away as is commonly supposed.

God's king is seen in David. He is the great precursor and figure of all God's thoughts for monarchy, and intentions in kingship, which he has purposed to be fulfilled in Christ. A king indeed. An absolute king. One whose sole word is the ultimate in law.

And as we have seen hitherto, first with David's manhood, next with his inheritance, and now with his majesty — prophetic, priestly and absolute — we are to note David's vastly significant relationship to Christ. Just as in all else, so in the matter of the throne and kingdom also, David prefigured the truth about his Messianic seed more clearly than any other person or any other teaching.

Now then, it follows that David in his dominion is a figure, and in his throne a picture, of that to be exercised and occupied by Christ.

There are two parts to the fulfilment of King David and his throne.

The first of these is heavenly and spiritual, and is fulfilled within Messiah's people in an interior way. This rule of Christ takes place now, in the present time.

The second, however, commences from the day of judgment, encompassing heaven and earth and all things seen and unseen. It reaches from this world to the next, from time to eternity. It will be consummated in the new creation, the new heavens and new earth, in the holy city, new Jerusalem come down from God out of heaven.

171

## The Son of God

### 1. The first fulfilment.

Consider the first way in which King David and his reign are fulfilled in Christ. It is in a way of the Spirit. It is fulfilled within his people in a spiritual way. It takes place at the present time. Now, at present, the rule of Christ is spiritual and heavenly.

Spiritual and heavenly, as David writes in Psalm 110, saying,

'The LORD said unto my Lord.'

That is, as we have before shown, the Father's speech to the Son, about to command the ascension:

'Sit thou at my right hand.'

Here is the ascension word itself. Christ sat down at the right hand of the Majesty on high. It is after the cross, after the three days in the tomb, after the forty days' resurrection. Then the ascension. That is the day on which these words foreheard by David in the Spirit of prophecy, actually came to pass. Ascension day.

But this is not the end of the speech. The Father continues to address the Son. It is about the matter of time. How long time shall he sit there?

'Until I make thine enemies thy footstool.'

*Psalm 110:1.*

Of course it is not so much a question of sitting literally. Sitting is indicative. It shows the king in a certain posture. It is a matter of reigning from the throne. Of being at rest, in his power, in the work which he has done, and in his ability to bring it to fruition. He sits as a king, reigning from the imperial and sovereign throne. It is that kind of sitting. For a limited period of time. Nevertheless a very long time. But it is not for ever. God limiteth a certain time, saying in David, 'Until.' Not for ever but until.

> 'Till all thine enemies be made thy footstool.'

When will that be?

It will not be till the day of judgment. The last day. The day of his wrath. The day of the great general resurrection to judgment described as the day when God will overwhelm all the earthly enemies and rejectors of Christ's rule and authority, making them his footstool.

> 'The Lord at thy right hand
> shall strike through kings
> in the day of his wrath.
> He shall judge among the heathen.
> He shall fill the places with the dead bodies.
> He shall wound the heads over many countries.'

> *Psalm 110:5,6.*

Here David foresees the last day, the day of judgment, the day of wrath. The vision is in terms of a great battle, a holocaust like that at Megiddo, an Armageddon. It is the picture of a final contest, a terrible day of slaughter of all the resisters of the Lord, the rebels against the king, the rejectors of his rule.

This prophetic vision is the picture taken up in Revelation chapters 16 and 19. It is God's judgment on

173

those that rejected the inward reign of Christ in time and during this life. It is in fact his judgment in the resurrection. This makes his enemies his footstool with a vengeance! He treads them all down, one by one.

Here then is the day in which all the Messiah's enemies are made to lie beneath his feet, his foot on the neck of the kings, judges and rulers. Thus they are made his footstool in fact. No 'until' about it, 'until' is past and the day has arrived up to which Christ had sat and waited patiently.

Nevertheless, the day of judgment is the last day. But between the day of ascension 'Sit thou,' and the last day 'the day of his wrath' there is this vast stretch of time in which we are found at present. During this age Christ sits reigning on high. In terms of the psalm this period began with the imperative of heaven 'Sit thou,' it is designated 'Until', and it concludes with the great day of wrath and of battle.

'Until.' We are in that period. It is the stretch of time bracketed between Christ's return to heaven and his second coming from heaven. It is now.

And in that period the question is, What is he doing? Clearly, as his posture indicates, he is reigning. Not at all over the world: the world is oblivious of him. Nevertheless he does reign. But how? He is active in ruling within his people by the Holy Ghost from heaven. That is what marks them out as his own: inward and spiritual submission.

Now briefly observe this in terms of Psalm 110:

*verse 1:*      opens with the ascension. The period during which Christ is ascended, commencing with the opening words and seen to extend over this present age. But not indefinitely. The period is circumscribed. 'Until.' Until the end of time.

*verses 2-4:*   These verses actually cover that period. The period between the ascension and the second coming. The present period. Now. During which Christ remains unseen, because he is in glory. As ascended, unseen, he remains sitting, reigning, on the right hand of the Majesty on high.

These three verses — verses 2, 3 and 4 — describe the actual exercise of Christ's present spiritual reign. This is a rule exclusively within, and can only be found in the interior of an inward people. As to Christ himself, he is in fact invisible.

This heavenly and spiritual reign commenced at Pentecost, it exists solely in the truly gathered saints indwelt by the Holy Ghost, and it continues till the last day.

It has continued now for two thousand years. Perhaps not so far hence it will conclude. But conclude it will.

*verses 5-6:*   These verses actually set forth the resurrection of the unjust, and the last judgment is graphically portrayed as a battlefield.

*verse 7:*   concludes the psalm with an insight into the king's resources. Not surprising, seeing that he has reigned in his saints these two thousand years already, and done so whilst unseen in heaven. How does he do it? He has a secret; David sees that.

Verse 7 describes the king's priestly and spiritual resources for so long and arduous a heavenly reign. Keeping his people over successive thousands of years, neither slumbering nor sleeping, generation by generation. Wonderful!

However does he do it? Whilst so high in heaven, and they so far below, amidst so many enemies on earth? He does it because of the wonderful resources at his disposal. He has this secret, you see.

So much then for this cursory and passing glance at Psalm 110. This will suffice as a general summary.

Our immediate object, however, is to proceed with the examination of verses 2-4 in particular. The present heavenly and spiritual reign of Christ, with which we are now concerned, appears in the following verses:

'The LORD shall send the rod of thy strength out of Zion: rule thou in the midst of thine enemies.
Thy people shall be willing in the day of thy power, in the beauties of holiness from the womb of the morning: thou hast the dew of thy youth.
The LORD hath sworn, and will not repent,

Thou art a priest for ever after the order of
Melchizedek.'

*Psalm 110:2-4.*

Whereas in verse 1 David narrates what he had heard
spoken between the Father and the Son — a prophecy
which was to come to pass on the day of ascension — now
the address changes. In the following three verses it is quite
different.

Here — verses 2 to 4 — it is not the Father addressing
the Son in the far distant future. It is David addressing the
Son. David is speaking to Christ in the spirit of prophecy.
David addresses the Son, in view of what he had heard in
the Spirit, and believed with understanding, about the
majesty of Christ.

Seeing this ascension, and hearing the Father's command, David now addresses his seed and his son. He speaks
in prophecy, admonition, comfort and assurance. This
prophetic counsel from David to his son is as a direct result
of his perceiving the ascension afar off, and therefore he
applies his words to Christ as ascended.

As a result, this entire passage — verses 2 to 4 — consists
of an exhortatory prophecy from King David to the future
seed of David when once that seed is raised from the dead
and seated in glory in the ascension.

Therefore these verses refer to Christ reigning from
heaven. Thus to the Son's present activity. They indicate
what he is doing now. He is not doing nothing. It is not
that he has finished his work on earth, and, ascended, has
nothing more to do from heaven. This is not a period of
inactivity for the Son. God forbid.

177

On the contrary, these prophetic verses indicate how very active the son of David is to be during the ascension period. That is, now. At the present time. From the day of ascension to the last day, the verses describe what Christ is to do. Then this passage tells us his precise activity at the present moment. Momentous truth! David begins with this assured promise to his son:

> 'The LORD shall send the rod of thy strength
> out of Zion.'
> *verse 2.*

Out of Zion? Zion? But the Messiah has just ascended. 'Sit thou at my right hand,' verse 1. Then, if just ascended, he is in heaven. And since it is evident, the rod of the king's strength goes forth from the place where he sits in majesty, how is he in Zion? We thought Zion to be David's city on earth, a part of Jerusalem.

Obviously then, David cannot be regarding the earthly location of Zion at Jerusalem. In prophecy he is regarding Zion in terms of the spiritual, divine and heavenly concepts associated with that city. That was what made Zion, and Jerusalem, important. And nothing but that.

Therefore David seeing this in Spirit, disassociates all that God had wrought in and spoken about Zion from the mere heap of bricks, stones, earth and rocks of that name. He sees that all that matters about Zion is what came down from God out of heaven in connection with that place.

Now, retaining the name so as to group every divine conception associated with the city of David, he leaves the bare earth, and ascends with these spiritual truths to the place where the king actually reigns.

And since it was the reign of the king that made the city of David what it was: then where the son of David is, there the true Zion exists in terms of all that is spiritual, heavenly and divine. After all, what else matters? David saw this, and said by the Spirit,

> 'The LORD shall send the rod of thy strength
> out of Zion.'

Zion. That is, *heavenly* Zion. From the setting of verse 1 this must be regarded as heavenly mount Zion, the 'hill of the Lord', that superior elevation to which the words 'Sit thou at my right hand' refer.

It is the place of ascension: the 'mount'. It is kingly rule in David: 'Zion'. It is the heavenly throne of the seed of David, 'ascended', as Peter says, 'into the heavens.' It answers to 'Jerusalem above', Galatians 4:26. 'Mount Sion, the city of the living God, the heavenly Jerusalem,' Hebrews 12:22. The city of the great king.

This is the place from which David assures Christ the king, Psalm 110:2, 'The LORD shall send the rod of thy strength.' That is, 'out of Zion.' Now from verse 1 we know that 'The LORD' refers to God and the Father, who commanded Christ's ascension. Therefore it is the Father who sends the rod of Christ the king's strength out of Zion.

Then what is 'the rod of thy strength'? Sent immediately after 'The LORD said unto my Lord, Sit thou at my right hand'? That is, after the ascension? Well, what is it that speaks of the rod — that is, authority — and strength — that is, power — of Christ, that the Father sent after the Son ascended up on high? That is, which was assured and promised of the Father in Psalm 110?

I answer, This refers to the person and work of the Holy Ghost. For ye shall receive power, saith he, after that the Holy Ghost is come upon you, Acts 1:8. With great power gave the apostles witness of the resurrection of the Lord Jesus, Acts 4:33. And again, I send the promise of my Father upon you: but tarry ye in the city of Jerusalem, until ye be endued with power from on high, Luke 24:49.

The strength of the ascended Son, David's Lord, stands in the power of the Holy Ghost. It is the Father's promise. God the Father speaks in prophecy by David, telling the newly ascended Son what he will do in consequence. 'Send the rod of Christ's strength.' And what is this but the promise of the Father obtained from heaven because of Christ's work on Calvary?

That is why it is said, 'made of the seed of David according to the flesh; and declared to be the Son of God *with power*, according to the spirit of holiness, *by the resurrection from the dead.'* The Son has power on earth effectively to accomplish his work from heaven. That is what he received, and sent, from the Father. Authority and power. Or, if you will, the rod of his strength.

What is Christ's strength to alarm, awaken, and convict the sinner? What calls the penitent to repentance? What is it that enables believing faith? Is it not light, life and love, invisibly and inwardly streaming from the Son of God in heaven? Is this not through the person and work of the Holy Ghost? Does not this command his sheep to follow him? And do they not, as from the dead, arise and do so? Is not this his authority and power? 'The rod of his strength'?

What is Christ's sanctifying and indwelling power but

the Holy Ghost here below? What constitutes the body of Christ but his indwelling? What else is the house of God but the temple of the Holy Ghost? What is the gathering and assembling power of Christ in his people but the uniting energies of the Holy Ghost? It is the Holy Ghost from heaven that constitutes the rod of Christ's strength.

Not the angels, though he commands them.

It is true that, the heavens being open, the angels are 'ascending and descending upon the Son of man,' John 1:51. Without angelic providences directed by the Son, how should we ever be prepared for his salvation? Without the angels of God, however should circumstances conspire to arrange that 'all things are now ready'?

How should the wayside, stony-ground, and thorny-ground believers ever have been turned into good ground perseverers, had it not been for the angels making ready for the Sower to sow the seed? How, without the angels of God, being directed, shutting up our way, and bringing those worldly disasters upon us which cause us to 'break up our fallow ground and sow not among thorns'?

Look at the angels' work with Cornelius and Peter. Remarkable. What ministers the angels are, ministering to the heirs of salvation. Wonderful their directed work. Work that pertains to Christ's use of providence and earthly circumstance to cause his people to turn to him alone, to own no other lord, to forsake all their idols, to call no man on earth 'father', to beware of the scribes and Pharisees.

How else should the obstacles be overcome to true and inward religion, unless, angelically, betimes they were forcibly removed? How else the distractions of financial dependence, earthly affections, natural relations, worldly ease and pleasure, unless smashed to pieces and ground to powder by the angels?

How else could we be strengthened to endure when crushed, broken, bruised, and discouraged beyond measure, the chastisement of years not yet ended? How else, except a little meal appeared, a cruse of water; so that we knew at last, at last, a providence from heaven? The angels.

But for all that, these things are not 'the rod of thy strength'. The angels are not Christ's authority and power amidst his people. The Holy Ghost himself is that, and his work is infinitely more inward and spiritual than the material concerns entrusted to angels under the command of Christ. The rod of Christ's strength is certainly not the angels: it is the Holy Ghost from heaven.

Clearly. The angels are plural. The rod of thy strength, is singular. It saith not Rods, as of many: but, 'the rod of thy strength', as of one. Singular, it refers to that by which the king on high rules within his people below: the Holy Ghost.

> 'The LORD shall send
> the rod of thy strength
> out of Zion:
> rule thou in the midst of thine enemies.'
>
> *Psalm 110:2.*

Then the Father's sending the rod of the Son's strength enables the Son to rule in the midst of his enemies?

Someone says, 'How can this be Christ ruling in the hearts of his people, as you say? They are not his enemies!'

I reply, Why do you not hold your peace until at least you have read what it says? It does not say that Christ rules his enemies. It says he rules *in the midst of* his enemies. An entirely different thing.

The rod of the Son's strength is sent so that from heaven, now, he may rule in the midst of his enemies. Not rule the enemies. Rule his people in the midst of countless enemies against that rule.

Precisely what you see in Acts. A separated, persecuted, sometimes beleaguered little company, yielded to Christ's rule, kept by the inward power of God, and waiting for his Son from heaven. The world raging around them, the religious of this world howling for their blood. Yet this lowly spiritually-minded company, filled with the Holy Ghost, looks for nothing but the world to come, joyfully sustained within by the heavenly rule of Christ from on high.

Now, this is Christ ruling in the midst of his enemies.

So then, the sending forth of the rod of the king's strength is the means by which Christ rules within his people here below. Not ruling the enemies. Ruling despite the enemies. And this he will do till the day of judgment. Then, all his enemies shall be made his footstool.

Now, enraged, the world and worldly religion must watch impotent as the absolute rule of the Son from heaven is obeyed, according to his own will, within the spiritual but despised company of his people. And who can let it? None.

And what is that will? To rule his people in the midst of

his enemies. And this, I say, is achieved by the indwelling Holy Ghost from heaven. He descends into the midst of Christ's enemies.

Observe:

*(i) Enemies interior to the believer in Christ.*

Within the body and soul of the saints. Here is a veritable legion of enemies, swift, cruel, and exceeding tenacious.

Inbred sin and all its allies. The natural mind. The unbelieving reason. The haughty intellect. The fleshly lusts. The worldly affections. The carnal passions. The proud heart. The stubborn will. The grasping ambitions. The self-righteous spirit. The deliberate darkness. All these allies swarm within as grasshoppers for multitude, a dreadful host.

However, they are not inbred sin. Inbred sin uses them. They say, as it were, 'It is no more I that do it, but sin that dwelleth in me,' Romans 7:17.

These are bad enough, and deep enough, themselves. But when all the might of deeper inbred sin roars and rages through them, one or any or some of them, they yawn and gasp insatiably. Or else with gentle subtlety, the deceitfulness of sin softly retires, curls up, hibernating, deep within the inmost lair of the soul. Who can know it?

'For I was alive without the law once: but when the commandment came, sin revived, and I died.' Roaring out of the cave, deep from within the lair it came, like a bear robbed of its whelps, furious that once more the captive soul had dared attend to true religion.

184

Enemies indeed, but the worst is not yet. Through inbred sin the hosts of darkness, the legions of demons and — if one were important enough in the kingdom — the principalities and powers, even Satan himself: all the legions of the diabolos, all whisper, strive, heave, thrust, intimidate, beg, coerce, bully, for the mastery. Enemies enough, within.

All these set themselves in array and take counsel together against the Lord and against his anointed. As long as the believer is in the body, for so long will these enemies maintain their implacable malevolence against him. Fleshly lusts that war against the soul, saith Peter, Abstain from them. They are incurable. Condemned in the flesh at the cross, through the suffering and crucifixion of Jesus, one must reckon oneself dead to them. But dead they are not, and depart they will not, till death and the resurrection.

They never cease to align themselves contrary to the Lord, and that in all manner of artful subtlety. Or once exposed, they will rage with terrible assault and battery. The tactics vary, but the strategy never.

Is the soul irreligious? Well; they will advance atheism. Is the soul religious? Excellent; they will advance hypocrisy. It must be they that reign and not the Holy Ghost. Whether outwardly religious or irreligious is by no means the criterion.

Who reigns within is the criterion. And it is consistent with an inward reign of the flesh, of inbred sin, of the devices and powers of Satan, quite consistent, I say, to have a great profession of scripture, a great show of evangelism, a great form of church dignity, and yet be under bondage to these aliens completely.

185

Who reigns within? That is the issue.

Satan will work through inbred sin and the flesh so long as it abideth. And it abides this life-long span. So long as the believer is in the body, inbred sin and the flesh abide also. And though the believer reckon himself dead to them by the cross, nevertheless they are there. And they are there contrary to the Spirit of God, and they are there as his remorseless and implacable enemy.

All these join themselves in battle array against — not the exterior scriptures, church, meetings, table, baptism, witness, religious works — against the reign of Christ within. Against the rule of the Spirit within. Against the triumph of the Spirit within.

'For the flesh lusteth against the Spirit, and the Spirit against the flesh' — within, that is; obviously within — 'and these are contrary the one to the other: so that ye cannot do the things that ye would,' Galatians 5:17.

No, you cannot, because ye must discriminate. It is not just what ye would, even when what ye would is outwardly religious. The Pharisees were outwardly religious. The question is, Who reigns within? From whence the inward motive: the flesh or the Spirit?

It is not just what ye would; even in religion, that is not trustworthy. It is a question of waiting on the Lord to discern from within what is of the flesh and what is of the Spirit. Who reigns? The flesh or the Spirit?

When the Lord shall send the rod of the king's strength out of Zion, saying, Rule thou in the midst of thine enemies, there is no doubt who reigns. The king reigns.

And he reigns by the power of the Spirit sent forth. The Spirit overcomes and triumphs over all the enemies within. All of them. And the heart meekly and gladly submits and bows before the king's sceptre.

Then comes to pass the saying that is written, Thy people shall be willing in the day of thy power. When the king reigns. When the Spirit rules.

Despite all the interior enemies, despite all the inward working of Satan and the hosts of darkness, then victory is obtained in the Lord's great name. The king asserting his sovereign right as absolute monarch, the Spirit poured out from on high to command his throne and sceptre within the people, overcoming is the inevitable consequence.

The Holy Ghost knows how to keep tender the broken and contrite heart — previously crushed by providences and shattered by convictions — that trembleth at his word. When this is so, for as long as it is so, the people are willing, they are willing, willing in the day of his power. Then Christ's reign is absolute. Absolutely.

When grace hath well refined the heart; when chastening hath long been endured to profit; when scourging hath made the wounded spirit tenfold the more sensitive and tender; when the felt and conscious fear of God softens the soul, keeps it serious, careful and low: then the king reigns. Then he reigns, not till then.

It is easily perceived, this inward reign. Very obvious, the marks are infallible: a serious people, sober and solemn, govern their joy with humility, their rejoicing with trembling.

Then, O Zion, behold! Rejoice greatly, O daughter of Jerusalem! Behold, thy king cometh unto thee, meek and lowly and riding upon an ass, and upon a colt, the foal of an ass. Then the king reigns. Then the naturally stubborn will breaks. Then the Spirit is shed forth in full renewal. Then 'Thy people shall be willing in the day of thy power.'

Then the interior reign of Christ the king. Then it is absolute. When the Spirit rules within the believer in the midst of his enemies.

### (ii) Enemies interior to the body of Christ.

Secondly, then, the rod of Christ's strength descendeth into the midst of the body of Christ to achieve discipline, enforce doctrine, bring in worship, and maintain the unity of that body.

Such a spiritual and true unity among the saints is nothing whatsoever to do with the uniting of various denominations together. Nor is it anything to do with the ecumenical movement determined upon being absorbed into the Roman Catholic church.

Furthermore, the oneness of the body of Christ is nothing to do with the delusion of unity which appears as a dream in the night when evangelicals from various denominations and ecumenical affiliations collect together, rejoicing in their evangelicalism for a week or two of evangelistic or convention ministry. Immediately thereafter they may be observed in different groups wending their way back to the places from which severally they came, and to which they elect to separate as a matter of fact.

Such behaviour — or rather misbehaviour — has no relation to the reign of Christ, no bearing on the rule of the Spirit, nothing in common with the unity of the body. Actually it is a flat contradiction to being all one in Christ Jesus. It is nothing but indifference to Christ. It is disobedience.

Another thing which — despite fond convictions to the contrary — has nothing to do with the unity of the body is present-day Brethrenism. Originally perhaps the most enlightened and spiritual movement since the early church, it was a work of God having its origin in the profound concern of noble-minded and deeply exercised Christians about this very question of unity.

Multitudes repudiated the whole principle of denominationalism. Great was the exercise about the nature of the church. In deep self-judgment, weeping and heart-broken with true humility, many came and returned into none other and no less than the unity of the one true body in Christ, to the fury and contempt of the professing church.

Alas! No longer. What obtained in the 1830's has long, long since departed. Present-day Brethren, rent and torn into more fragments than the sum of all the denominations from which originally they withdrew, now bear no relation to the original.

Of course, in no case do I speak of the piety of the individual. It is consistently the movement to which I refer.

Whereas in the early eighteen hundreds, the first cause was a departure from sectarianism and return into the unity of the body, now in the late nineteen hundreds, the denominations are far less sectarian than the Brethren themselves. And over less petty and ignoble trifles than outward forms and notions. Or outdated and irrelevant clashes and issues between themselves.

In Victorian times the Brethren fathers must needs leave the denominations to unite with those gathered into one body. Today, the sons of those fathers needs must leave the divisions of Brethrenism if they wish to follow in their early fathers' footsteps.

Modern Brethrenism may be obsessed with its paltry — unspiritual and unscriptural — penurious criteria: 'Breaking of bread on Lord's day morning'; the substitution of any-man ministry — no matter the drivel spoken — in place of the execrated 'one-man ministry'. It may be the harbour of false-assurance, easy-believism, dangerous pre-millennial dispensationalism, and doctrine-less meandering. It may. But it is certainly nothing to do with the unity of the body of Christ.

The rod of Christ's strength appears in relation to the unity of the body, as and when the saints return to him with mourning, weeping, and contrition. When they return to him with meltedness and brokenness of heart.

Return, that is, from all their party spirit, division, and sectarianism. Return from all the haughty traditionalism, the devised creeds, the systems of doctrine arranged by men. From all the forms of meetings, forms of the church, forms of ordinances, that hitherto divided them.

Return from sects organised over partial truths, from divisions owing their existence to isolated ordinances, such as baptism, the 'breaking of bread', the Lord's supper. Return from denominations formed by the rise of strong personalities. Return from arguments held by the mind, doctrines formed in the intellect, traditions received from the fathers. Return from churches formed by independency, presbytery, episcopacy, anarchy. Return from divisions over church government, no government, over ministerial systems, no ministerial systems, over some favourite preacher, over no preacher at all.

Return to the reign within. Return to the Holy Ghost within. Return to God and the Father within. Return to the Lord.

It is not a question of peripheral views, or the formation of theological creeds, or the devising of doctrinal philosophies. The gospel itself, the faith once delivered, is the sole and sufficient body of doctrine to be held. But even so, even with the simplicity of the gospel, first and foremost it is a question of power. The Lord's power. Thy people shall be willing in the day of thy power. That gathers. Everything else scatters.

The Lord shall send the rod of thy strength out of Zion. Rule thou in the midst of thine enemies. Thy people shall be willing in the day of thy power. Willing to overcome the enemies. The enemies that divide, separate, and denominate the actual and true members of the body.

Spiritual enemies that have first divided the body, then scattered the separated members far apart. Not content with this, these enemies have further engineered the scattered fragments of the one body into a bewildering variety of worldly congregations in which the members of Christ form but a minute percentage. A minute percentage, that is, of the whole. Of unconverted congregations met and gathered on principles of denomination clean contrary to the word of God and commandment of the Lord. And in any event denominations which are also severally divided among themselves.

What confusion! 'Arise, O Lord, let thine enemies be scattered.'

Thy people shall be willing in the day of thy power. Yes, that is so. But not without a battle.

Oh! With what apostolic labours wrestled the servants of the Lord at the time of the Acts of the apostles, what labours to unite the saints and keep them in the unity of the one body.

At Corinth and Rome, at Colosse and Ephesus, in Galatia and Thessalonica, we mark the fervent prayers, the strong crying and tears, ever ascending to heaven. We perceive the kindled, burning, melted, anointed preaching; the earnest pleading, the crying, exhortation, the labour, and devotion, the spirituality of teaching.

How warm, how experimental, how on fire were these ministers of God for the perfection of the saints, the edification of the body, and the intelligent, interior and exterior unity of all the members.

And these things being so, shall the unity of the body be recovered and maintained with less than these fervent labours?

For there is one body. And as baptised into that body by one Spirit, meek and obedient, the saints submit within. Then Christ rules in the midst of his enemies. He reigns, when 'In the midst of the assembly will I sing praise unto thee.' And when 'No man among you thinketh of himself more highly than he ought to think.' Then, 'The body maketh increase unto the edifying of itself in love.'

That is, when all accept the mortification of the flesh, of the deeds of the body, by the Spirit. When all accept each one with joy; accept the limitations of one's own measure and gift without envy of those with greater, or contempt for those with less. But all as brethren together in one, as saints drinking into one Spirit, all contributing in the measure of their faith according to grace given, denying the flesh, shutting out the world, all moved by one Spirit.

Then, though the world, the false church, worldly religion, disobedient brethren too, conspire against the gathered saints, raging against them from without, still Christ reigns within and stands in the midst. The rod of his strength goes forth out of Zion.

Christ reigns! Absolutely. Among gathered saints; not gathered to notions, but in the Holy Ghost. Not gathered to systems of doctrine, but the interior power of Christ. Not gathered to a sectarian name or advocate, but to the Father. Then, Christ reigns. And power is known in the gospel. Then, he rules in the midst of his enemies.

This kingly rule is absolute. It is from heaven. It is spiritual. It is made known in the heart, within the interior. But one says, Can it happen? What a disgraceful saying! What dreadful unbelief! Is he not crowned on high? Is he not king? Doth he not reign?

Yes! It both happened and will happen again. For,

'Thy people *shall* be willing in the day of thy power,'

saith the Father Almighty to Christ, and this saying holds good throughout the age. It echoes and rings down to this present time, appealing to all believing people today. Today, if ye will hear his voice, harden not your hearts.

But must we wait inert till the day of his power to 'depart from iniquity'? From clericalism, sectarianism, denominationalism, brethrenism, independent missionism, anarchy, from the creeds, systems, theologies of men, the divisions, traditions and barriers, which men erect?

No; for 'the day of thy power' in verse 3, is synonymous with the 'Sit thou' of verse 1. It is commensurate with the ascension. It is 'until' the 'day of his wrath', verse 5, therefore, throughout this era.

It is 'the Lord's day' of this whole age, a day marked by the rising of the Son in his heavenly ascension. Within the true meaning of 'the Lord's day', this is a day to rise up by faith. It is the day that the Lord hath made: let us be glad and rejoice in it. Let us first believe; then pray; and finally expect.

It is not waiting that is needed; it is praying. It is not passivity that is required; it is personal repentance. It is not waiting on the Lord in a place that dishonours him; it is contrition to be united in the place where his honour dwells. Personal and united penitence is required. 'Save yourselves from this untoward generation!' That is the word. That is what is needed.

Real separation within unto the Spirit's rule for Christ. Real heart submission to his reign from on high. And true separation without, from all that divides us from the body, and the body from us, and which divides the body in itself.

Yieldedness. That is needed. How wretched the rebellious hardness of heart and fleshly false loyalties that divide the true saints from the unity of the body, from gathering to Christ alone.

But when this is put away, all this is put away, then, 'Thy kingdom come.' Then, behold, 'The kingdom of God is within you.' Then, 'The kingdom of God is not meat and drink' — no, neither creed-making nor form-following — 'but righteousness, and peace, and joy in the Holy Ghost.' Then 'Yours is the kingdom of God.' Then, his heavenly kingly reign is absolute indeed.

Then spirituality, heavenliness, humility, awe, the fear of God, the love of the brethren, compassion, kindness, preferring one another; then the power of the Lord, the presence of God, the outpouring of the Spirit; then the freshness, the immediacy, the instant sense: 'The Lord is there!' Then his reign is absolute.

This being his day, only sinful ignorance, stubbornness and rebellion, prevent what otherwise must happen of course. Then let us repent and truly return. Let us, brethren, let us appear in our own day a living testimony to the day of his power: a present demonstration that *he is an absolute king.*

### 2. The last fulfilment.

The second and final way in which King David and his throne are seen to be fulfilled in Christ is more far-reaching than the first.

It commences from the day of judgment, encompasses

heaven and earth and all things seen and unseen. It reaches from the end of this world endlessly into the next. It is ushered in at the last day of time and extends to timeless eternity. It will find its consummation in the new creation, the new heavens and new earth, in the holy city, new Jerusalem come down from God out of heaven.

But however could all this be depicted in David?

Well, of course, but dimly. Dimly, as in all the types and figures. Naturally, at best they are but shadows which had stretched beforehand along the path of time. They had no substance, no dimension, no reality. They were the shadow cast by the light of reality.

Nevertheless, however flat they fell, their shape was still taken from the outline of that figure of whom they were the forerunners and from whose light they derived their existence.

Only the shadow of good things to come. Then did they mind such obscurity? No. They didn't mind. They were not obsessed with their ministry, but his. They had no self-interest, they were lost in the interests of the king. For them to have lived was a privilege, and for them to live was Christ.

Yet mere shadows? Only forerunners? Yes, but of whom? That is what makes the difference. Makes easy the denial of self, the forgetfulness of one's own existence, the dismissal of self-centred service, the spurning of self-indulged ministry, the contemptuous trampling on self-glorious display. More than easy: it was a pleasure. 'He must increase, but I must decrease,' saith the Forerunner, John 3:27-30.

David, then, in his past kingdom was a shadow of Christ in his coming dominion. Only a shadow, yes. But still, the outline was there. But where?

We have before shown that the promise to Abraham of a seed in Canaan the land of promise depicted Christ and the inheritance of the world to come. Therefore it follows that in like manner David's throne in Canaan depicted Christ's future kingly reign over that coming world.

First, we have seen the inheritance of the world to come typified in Abraham and the land of promise. Now on the same basis we are to see the throne over that coming world itself depicted in King David ruling upon Mount Zion. Both are seen to be fulfilled in Christ. Of course. He is the son of Abraham: the heir. And he is the son of David: the king.

Moreover, this does not depend upon man, no, not even upon the son of David himself:

> 'For the Lord God shall give unto him
> the throne of his father David,
> and of his kingdom there shall be no end.'

The throne of his father David? David the king occupied the throne established upon Mount Zion, at Jerusalem, reigning over all the land of Israel. Is no more than this, then, the throne which Christ inherits? Literally, a replica of King David's throne?

By no means. For just as we have seen that the land of Israel was a figure of that better country, the heavenly land of promise, the world to come whereof we speak: so also is the throne of David.

197

The throne which David occupied upon Mount Zion at Jerusalem reigning over all the land of Israel, must be seen as a figure. It typified the coming throne of Messiah the king reigning in the holy city, the heavenly Jerusalem, exercising his dominion over all that new creation, the new heavens and earth, the universe to come, world without end. Amen.

The throne of David in Jerusalem was a figure for the time then present of the claim of God for his future king to a coming world dominion.

Of course there are certain who suppose that Christ will one day literally occupy David's throne in Israel. They take David's throne in the literal sense. How puerile! Ridiculous. The one to occupy David's throne is David. And the one to occupy Christ's throne is Christ. Of which David and his throne were the figures.

Ridiculous, to admit of David as being a type, forthwith to deny David's throne as a figure. Such people should make up their minds: it is one way or the other.

If in the resurrection, David's throne is literal, then it was never a figure. And if not, then neither was David. And where are they now? This way they arrive at David himself on the throne in the world to come! But if it once be admitted that David himself was a type, then it follows his throne *must* have been a figure also.

Whether is greater: the throne, or him that sits on the throne? If the occupant of Zion's throne was a type of the king to come, then of course, the throne which the type occupied must be figurative too. The alternative of a literal throne and a typical David, is absurd.

If the king is a type, then so is the throne of his kingdom. Now, the throne of Christ must be that much greater than David's, the kingdom of Christ that much superior to Israel, precisely in the proportion that Jesus Christ the Son of God, the seed of David, the King of kings, himself exceeds King David in stature.

Of necessity, just as King David was nothing but a shadow of the radiant ascendancy of the glorious majesty of the King of kings: equally the throne on Mount Zion in Israel was no more than a mere shade of the everlasting glory, of the untold dominion, of that wonderful throne resplendent in the kingdom of God.

'But unto the Son he saith,
Thy throne, O God,
is for ever and ever.'

*Hebrews 1:8.*

Now of the things which we have spoken this is the sum: The throne upon Mount Zion was a figure in David of the future claim on the part of God's elect, the Messiah, to absolute world dominion. However, that dominion is not destined to be established in the world as now constituted, which hath an end.

Of necessity any dominion in the world during this present age must be curtailed at the last day, the day of judgment. Then it must end. Then it is finished.

But Christ's dominion, which is endless, cannot finish; therefore it cannot be established in this passing world. For of his dominion there shall be no end; his kingdom is an everlasting kingdom; his reign is in a world, world without end. Therefore it cannot possibly pertain to the world that now is, because when it comes it comes without any limitation; but this world has every limitation. Observe:

> 'The heavens and the earth,
> which are now,
> by the same word are kept in store,
> reserved unto fire
> against the day of judgment
> and perdition of ungodly men.
> But the day of the Lord will come
> as a thief in the night;
> in the which the heavens shall pass away
> with a great noise,
> and the elements shall melt
> with fervent heat,
> the earth also and the works that are therein
> shall be burned up.
> The heavens being on fire
> shall be dissolved,
> and the elements shall melt
> with fervent heat.
> Nevertheless we,
> according to his promise,
> look for new heavens and a new earth,
> wherein dwelleth righteousness.'

*II Peter 3:7,10,12,13.*

Therefore the earth that Christ shall inherit is that which first shall have passed through the fiery deluge. The dominion which he shall establish shall be after the great conflagration, and in the resurrection in the world to come.

This in no way alters the crown rights of the King of

kings to the present world: it shows simply that those rights are actually taken up after the world has been purified in the judgment and changed by the purging fire. How suitable to the inheritance of the Son of God. Pure.

God never relinquished the earth. His claim was ever asserted. 'The earth is the LORD'S, and the fulness thereof.' But men filled it with wickedness, soiled it with filth, mired it with iniquity, ingrained it with dirt, and their works they have reared — generation by generation — reared as a tower to heaven.

And this is Christ's inheritance? This earth, this world?

Yes, when the works thereof are burned up with fire; yes, when the self-same heavens and earth have passed through the all-purifying, all-dissolving, elemental fire of the last day.

Then. Then he shall inherit, and establish the kingdom. But not till then. How suitable this is, to the inheritance of the Son of God, world without end.

From the foregoing it will be seen that we repudiate with vigour the bewildering schemes dreamed up against the truth by those premillennial somnambulists, who wander aimlessly through Revelation chapter twenty.

Not only have their complicated wanderings bewitched many easily led brethren, but the irresponsible juggling of these chiliastic conjurers has captivated attention away from the wreckage of the truth strewn in their pathway.

And should they now begin to murmur and mumble at me to fetch them proof of my assertions, if God will, they shall not be disappointed. But they will wish they had held their peace.

Sufficient unto the day, then, we have shown clearly from the principles established, that there can be no physical, or material, reign of Christ on the earth as now constituted. The very idea of a thousand-year Judaistic reign from Jerusalem in this present world after some secret rapture and third — third! — coming of Christ, is not only ridiculous: it is thoroughly erroneous and dangerous.

The truth is that this world shall continue till the last day, which is the day of Christ's return, the day of the rapture, the day of judgment, and the day of the dissolution and fiery conflagration of all things, as Peter teaches. After all this forthwith appears the world to come, the new heavens and new earth, the holy city, new Jerusalem, and the everlasting kingdom world without end.

This is when the Son establishes his inheritance for ever, and when the King of kings commences the reign of his dominion which shall have no end, from age to age to eternity. Amen.

Since the ancient enemy, Satan, contests all these rights and every position destined for Christ, it follows that in the last analysis world dominion is the ultimate issue of this conflict. Because world dominion must be the final vindication of God's chosen Messiah. That is what is contested. And what has been contested, from the fall up to the present day.

The age-long conflict is drawn up to the battle lines: to whom shall be the spoils of world rule? Whose the crown of world dominion?

The acute intelligence of diabolos has no illusions about the title 'King of the Jews'. And, whatever the myopic dimness of millennialists — who, to the delight of the Deceiver, cannot see afar off — Satan himself does not limit the throne of David, nor does he attenuate the true meaning of the promised land of Israel.

The Adversary from the beginning was ever aware that the advent of the 'seed of David according to the flesh' heralded war in heaven. He perceived the fundamental importance of this event. He knew that Jesus was God's predestined king, and if so, heir to all the dominions over which claim had been made.

This struck him to the very heart. 'Where is he that is born King of the Jews?' He sees the threat to all that his heart desired. World rule. That is the issue of heaven.

Now these truths bring out the greatness of God's purpose and wisdom. In the beginning God entrusted the earth to Adam, created in the image of God to be nourished by and subject to his only-begotten Son, for whose glory everything had been created and made. Set forth as the Tree of Life, the Son was central to all God's purposes in manhood.

He was the purpose, without whom was not anything made that was made. He was before all things; all things were made by him, and by him all things consist.

He was the reason for being; and creation awaited the unfolding of divine counsels in the coming manifestation of the Son of God. It was not yet, but it was to come.

He was the light of men.

Sustained by the nourishment of his divine presence — signified by the tree of life — Adam awaited the consummate fulfilment of God's purpose, the crowning glory of all things. There was no thought that this had been reached in himself. No thought that creation's glory was yet complete.

Everything was for the One that should come; for the manifestation of him for whom all that had been made was made. He was the firstborn of every creature. In him was life. The Son was the light of creation.

Dependent upon his invisible but typified presence, man tilled the ground, kept the garden, replenished the earth, subdued it, and began the exercise of that dominion which he should maintain by the unseen presence of the awaited and coming Son of God.

So it was in that day when God formed man of the dust of the ground, and breathed into his nostrils the breath of life. And man became a living soul. God created man in his own image; in the image of God created he him; male and female created he them.

God blessed them. God said to them, Be fruitful, multiply, have dominion. All that man required for nourishment and sustenance, in body and soul, was found in the garden. Fair it was in that day. It was very good.

But man fell. The tempter entered the garden and deceived the woman, who tempted the man, and both were found in the great transgression.

Adam rebelled against God, loved darkness rather than light, and brought in the reign of sin and death. Now there could be no question of dominion in and through man. Therefore the seriousness of the fall cannot be overstated.

Man's own departure, as well as the withdrawal of God, together with the judgment, had a profound interior effect.

Man himself came under thraldom. Now enslaved to the passions, lusts, desires and affections, these in their turn were in bondage to inbred sin, the will no longer free. This was the generation of mankind. Their hearts were blinded; the understanding turned to vanity; the light waned; darkness settled.

Nor was this all. The tempter having achieved his immediate purpose through the fall, departed neither this world nor that humanity doomed beneath his sway. Rather, he consolidated his victory, concentrated his forces, and maintained his objective. Yet with so light a touch that forgetful man soon became unaware of his existence.

With superior subtlety Satan ruled the following ages of mankind, leading the nations at his own will. Nor was this captivity one of exterior influence and persuasion as it had been in the temptation. Now captivity lay within. It was in the life of mankind, in the generation of man. The power lay deep within.

'Ye are of your father the devil, and the lusts
of your father ye will do. He was a murderer
from the beginning, and abode not in the
truth, because there is no truth in him. When
he speaketh a lie, he speaketh of his own:
for he is a liar, and the father of it.'

*John 8:44.*

In the life of man, from the seed of Adam, the father of mankind. But, fallen, not the only father: 'Ye are of your father the devil.' In the life, this poison. Spread to every generation and all the race.

Hence it is said, 'The whole world lieth in wickedness.' 'He deceiveth the whole world.' So much so that Satan, or diabolos, is called 'the god of this world', who blinds the unbelieving nations. A veil lies upon the face of all people, and as to the individual, lo, Satan hath bound him these many years. Since how long came this upon him? 'Of a child.' Estranged from the womb. It is a matter of origins.

But of this, mankind is oblivious. Oblivious. Mankind is born oblivious to this origin, and, deceived, is careless to discover the dreadful cause. Yet on every hand and everywhere the symptoms crowd in upon him and cry for diagnosis. It is a great, but a willing delusion. 'Men loved darkness rather than light,' John 3:19.

Thus men are born to disobedience. 'Sons of disobedience,' Ephesians 2:2. Therefore disobedience was in the blood before they existed: disobedience was their father, that is the origin; and true to nature, man never disappoints the description.

A child of wrath also, that is his nativity, impending wrath, a city of destruction: the cry should ring in his ears, 'Flee from the wrath to come!' But does it? Far from it, man's ears are heavy. Being dead in sins, he hears nothing, but with vain thoughts of freedom saunters heedlessly into eternity, whilst enslaved completely to 'the course of this world'.

This course is wholly in the power, and precisely at the

direction, of 'the prince of the power of the air', yet another descriptive name for Satan. But to him, and to his powers invisible, men remain both dead and insensible, slumbering on till the day of slaughter.

Then how completely Satan rules humanity! Unknown and imperceptible. The world held captive at his own will.

Wherefore? To what end? The end of his will and of all his strife remains what it was from the beginning: the achievement of totalitarian control through the unification of the world state and world religion under the Man of his own appointment. The world ruler.

But God disappoints this desire. Frustrating Satan's pride, God asserts the right of his elect king to the dominion of the earth. He is the one for whom all things were created. No matter what has entered the world; despite the fall; God's purposes stand sure. Far from admitting to Satan's assumptions, nothing at all is yielded. The earth, saith he, The earth is the LORD'S, and the fulness thereof.

However Satan, under his title 'The prince of this world', pretends to its throne. Not in his own person; he is an interior, invisible spirit; but in that Man who is the embodiment of all his diabolical subtlety, of all his bewitching delusion, Satan will raise up the head. He will come to the kingdom.

When this comes to pass, shall perception, shall faith be found — or if found, permitted — in the earth? At such a time how ready the world is for this saviour, a messiah worthy of its accommodation. Truly, all things are now ready.

All things are now ready. But not for the anointed Saviour of God. Not for the true Lord Jesus. Not for the elect Messiah. Although, deceitfully, the titles 'Jesus', 'Christ', and so on, are transposed by the cunning Adversary to another Jesus, a false Christ, one which accommodates every worldliness, every looseness, every lawlessness. Suited to the sons of disobedience. This pleases foolish humanity.

But what man cannot see, his eyes being blinded, what he cannot see is the vast concentration of swiftly moving forces flowing through the life of all humanity, moving all unaware to the final climax.

The god of this world audaciously contests the throne; he counters the claim of every office of God's Messiah. Through fallen man and the ungodly nations, the Deceiver proclaims the contrary to pure and astringent gospel truth; he corrupts the gospel to suit every self-indulgence and worldly lust whilst retaining much of its vocabulary. He proclaims the contrary, I say, ever striving for world dominion, deceiving mankind through their yielded assent to the ideal of one unified domination over all peoples.

For all that comes up from the earth, all that ascends from man, and all that arises from the world, helps forward his purpose.

However nothing that comes down from heaven, nothing that descends from God, nothing that is outpoured from the Holy Ghost, does anything but frustrate his purpose. It confounds and confuses the prince of this world.

This is the cause of Satan's discomfort at the promise of God to Abraham, that he should inherit the land of

Canaan. Because Canaan, promised to Abraham and his seed, shows that God ignores Satan's claims. A word was dropped from heaven, the Lord of hosts asserted this right from on high:

'God hath spoken in his holiness;
I will rejoice,
I will divide Shechem,
and mete out the valley of Succoth.
Gilead is mine,
and Manasseh is mine;
Ephraim also is the strength of mine head;
Judah is my lawgiver.'

*Psalm 60:6,7.*

It is his. He lays claim to the land from the top to the bottom. It is not yet the whole earth; it is a claim, a reservation; it is a token: but if that is his, all is his. And if so, then God contemptuously brushes aside all that the god of this world had so carefully established.

That is the significance of Canaan. That is what Paul saw in the promise of Canaan to Abraham:

'The promise that he should be
the heir of the world.'

*Romans 4:13.*

That is what Canaan represented: God's claim to the earth; he says to Abraham, 'To thee will I give it.' How this must have enraged Satan, after all that he thought he had established for ever. Saith God to Abraham, To thee will I give it.

209

Nevertheless, Satan would not relinquish what he had established through the unfaithfulness and rebellion of man, and he set about the corruption of Abraham's seed. But the truth is, he never knew the meaning of Abraham's seed, any more than he understood the ultimate and heavenly significance of Canaan. Why not? Because he is a premillennialist and the father of it.

Every time and at each turn, frustrated and enraged, Satan missed the whole meaning of the work of God from heaven. God on high moved sublimely over all that the Adversary had achieved below, as if it had not occurred, and as if Satan did not exist.

'O the depth of the riches
both of the wisdom and knowledge of God!
How unsearchable are his judgments,
and his ways past finding out!
For who hath known the mind of the Lord?
Or who hath been his counseller?
Or who hath first given to him,
and it shall be recompensed unto him again?
For of him, and through him, and to him,
are all things:
to whom be glory for ever. Amen.'

*Romans 11:33-36.*

And if Satan raged over the promise of Canaan, how much more over the throne of David in the land of Canaan? For when God established a throne in David and assured the king that his dominion should know no end, that the heathen were his for the asking, and that he should reign from shore to shore: we may be certain that Satan, having great wrath, veritably fell from heaven as lightning in his anger, swift to the contest.

For now it is not a parcel of ground between Egypt and Mesopotamia. Now it is everything. Everything, that is, everything that had been lost through Adam's great transgression.

The figure of the promises given to Abraham shows that everything that had been lost will be reclaimed by judgment and in resurrection. And the figure of the throne of David shows that the king whom Satan strove to usurp, God will establish in the world to come, world without end. Amen.

And absolutely everything will be recovered. Everything. Everything in its entirety.

Boundless in his wrath, the god of this world storms through his fading domain, stirring the world to a fury against God's purpose, but

> 'Why do the heathen rage,
> and the people imagine a vain thing?
> The kings of the earth set themselves,
> and the rulers take counsel together,
> against the LORD,
> and against his anointed,
> saying, Let us break their bands asunder,
> and cast away their cords from us.'
>
> *Psalm 2:1-3.*

This quotation shows clearly that when God raises up the throne of David in Zion, seeing — though not seeing aright — the significance of this, Satan becomes frenzied. His winds lash the waves, the floods lift up their voice, they lift up their voice, they make a mighty noise. They rage together.

Yet despite the rulers of the earth; the kings of the nations; the tumultuous peoples; the course of this world; the prince of the power of the air; the world rulers of this darkness; the spiritual wickedness in the heavenly places: despite it all.

Despite the progress of humanity; the increase of knowledge; the achievements of civilisation; the overcoming of barriers; the reaching for the stars; the attainment of the near-impossible; the incredible advances of men: despite it all.

Despite the apostasy of the church; the collapse of Christendom; the failure of the testimony; the scattering of the flock; the withholding of the word of the Lord; the quenching of the Spirit; the absence of prophetic ministry; the rise of pseudo-evangelicalism; the flood of easy-believism; the coming of the world church: despite it all.

Despite so apparently invincible a combination on the earth and over the earth, and from the earth, God responds on this wise:

> 'He that sitteth in the heavens shall laugh:
> the LORD shall have them in derision.
> Then shall he speak unto them in his wrath,
> and vex them in his sore displeasure.
> Yet.'

Yet; despite it all. Yet, that is, until a given time. Till the last day, the day of judgment, the day of wrath, the final conflict. Till then, on the throne in the heavens, invisibly in the glory, till the very last day,

> 'Yet have I set my king upon
> my holy hill of Zion.'

*Psalm 2:4-6.*

And what that means is this: By the throne in the heavens, and him that sits thereon, God gives notice that what is signified in the throne of David shall surely, but surely, surely come to pass.

His seed shall inherit the earth. His king shall govern the world. To the son of David is the throne of dominion, for he is worthy to receive power, and riches, and wisdom, and strength. He shall most assuredly rule from the throne of the everlasting kingdom.

Blessing and honour and glory and power, be unto him that sitteth upon the throne, and unto the Lamb for ever and ever. Amen.

Now unto the King eternal, immortal, invisible, the only wise God, be honour and glory for ever and ever. Amen.

Invisible; at present invisible. Nevertheless, in his times he shall show who is the blessed and only Potentate, the King of kings and Lord of lords; who only hath immortality, dwelling in the light which no man can approach unto; whom no man hath seen, nor can see: to whom be honour and power everlasting. Amen.

So then, it is with abundant testimony that God bears record before all the world to the coming kingdom.

The present visible absence of Christ, his reign from glory, his impending return to judgment, all bespeak the danger and solemnity of neglecting this royal issue. Total allegiance is heralded. Misplaced loyalty appears out of court. 'To wait for his Son from heaven' is the closing counsel of the apostolic labours bestowed upon the church of God, I Thessalonians 1:10.

Then surely the world will give the more earnest heed to this coming king and the heavenly kingdom?

No, they will not.

Before the flood they would not. Does one object, Christ had not then come, how could his throne have been rejected? I reply, Because the king is immortal, invisible, God only wise. Because the throne is eternal in the heavens.

Enoch warned the old world. The Lord cometh! he cried. But they would not. What folly. The guilt of rebellion increases in direct proportion as the rank of authority rises. The eternal weight of that ultimate divine Majesty against which the world then rebelled may be gauged by the retributive fury of the overwhelming flood. *

At the tower of Babel they would not. Rather than submit to the throne of God and the promised king, they challenged the throne and rejected the king.

About this time Nimrod led the world. He began to be a mighty one in the earth. The world followed him with admiration, they spoke of him with admiration. Yet he was

---

* See 'Noah and the Flood'. The Publishing Trust, price 60p.

nothing but a rebel before the Lord. But, alas! This was what appealed to them: the daring of his rebellion and lawlessness against the throne. So they spoke of him; their speech became proverbial, as it is said, Even as Nimrod the mighty 'hunter' before the Lord.

Pharaoh was another who rebelled against the throne, yet all the world wondered after him in those days. But he would not, he would not, he just would not submit to the Lord. Yet the world followed him, neither could they be deterred, nor persuaded to change their allegiance, no, not even when Pharaoh and all his host perished beneath the waters of the Red Sea.

Indeed, appalling as the fact appears, it is still a fact that for all the time that passed, not one of the kings of the earth ruled for God till the days of King David. That is, except for the mystical figure of Melchizedek King of Salem.

However the throne of David was in complete submission to the throne of God, and therefore it follows that the one was a true representation of the other before all Israel. The throne of David was a faithful though pale reflection of that invisible and eternal throne in the heavens. And what is seen? That that throne claims the earth.

'The heaven is my throne, and the earth is my footstool,' saith the Lord. Echoes David, 'The heavens are thine, the earth also is thine: as for the world and the fulness thereof, thou hast founded them. The north and the south, thou hast created them.' He understood all this.

He goes on, 'Justice and judgment are the habitation of thy throne, mercy and truth shall go before thy face.'

David not only understands God's throne, but he embodies divine claims to the earth. 'Once have I sworn by my holiness that I will not lie unto David. His seed shall endure for ever, and his throne as the sun before me.' David reflected in his throne that Majesty on high.

The throne upon Mount Zion at Jerusalem declares that God refuses the verdict of the kings of the earth. He denounces what man has done to his creation by the fall. He rejects the sentence passed against his rule by the world. The throne on Mount Zion shows in David that God will not relinquish his right to rule the world.

The truth is that the throne in Canaan represents God's claim to the earth. He refuses the verdict of men, the world, and the god of this world. It is mine, saith the Lord.

And he shall receive it. The throne and its associate promises show this. He says to David, Thy seed will I establish for ever, and build up thy throne to all generations. Selah. The meek shall inherit the earth. Saith he concerning the son of David, Of his kingdom there shall be no end.

Therefore David's throne signifies God's right to world dominion just as the land of Canaan represents God's claim to the world itself.

The throne of David typified world dominion. That is what is in the mind of God, no less; that is what he is teaching, that is what is in view.

Because that is what was lost. That is what Adam forfeited. It is that of which man in Adam has judged himself unworthy. From the beginning, at the fall, the world was given over to the prince of this world, and that deceitful spirit will assert in man his own influential world rule and dominion. That is what has been, and it is what is coming yet again.

Satan knows that the earth is promised to the seed of David, but he contests it: he exerts all his invisible and vast forces, he gathers his powers, he sends his spiritual energies into all the world. Unknown to that world.

The origin of such an urgent movement towards world government, men suppose, lies within themselves. But it does not. That is not the origin. No, it is the intangible, invisible, imperceptible influence of that being who has consistently pursued this single aim from the beginning.

One world, one people, one tongue, one government, one ruler. One world throne. It is world dominion by that man whom the god of this world chooses. The man he forwards as most representative of his own beguiling ingenuity, his own extraordinary ability, his own facile transformation of himself to appear as the epitome of all that is good and optimistic in a world that has never been more in need of hope.

Moreover, such a choice of Satan will reflect his own deceit and diabolical subtlety in misrepresenting the throne of God. And, as regards the few poor scattered saints and congregations — that remain submissive and faithful to the throne in heaven — they will be misconstrued as being damaging, antisocial and downright destructive of the commonwealth.

And if this should seem a thing incredible to men, let them hear the prophecy of no less an authority than the

217

apostle Paul, writing some two thousand years ago of events now beginning to take place about us:

> 'For the mystery of iniquity doth already work:
> only he who now letteth will let,
> until he be taken out of the way.
> And then shall that Wicked be revealed,
> whom the Lord shall consume
> with the spirit of his mouth,
> and shall destroy
> with the brightness of his coming:
> Even him,
> whose coming is after the working of Satan
> with all power and signs and lying wonders,
> And with all deceivableness of unrighteousness
> in them that perish;
> because they received not the love of the truth,
> that they might be saved.'

*II Thessalonians 2:7-10.*

Furthermore, as to the appearance of him whom Satan will choose to present to the world, and the conditions that precede this manifestation, let no one think that it will be lewd, irreligious, or without the appearance and claim both to being of God, and Christian:

> 'Let no man deceive you by any means:
> for that day shall not come,
> except there come a falling away first,
> and that man of sin be revealed,
> the son of perdition.'

Son of perdition. Used in only one other place, John 17:12, this is the name for Judas, one of the twelve apostles. Not that the man of whom Paul prophesied could be he, obviously, but the name indicates a false apostle at the very head of the church, which by now, observe, has 'fallen away first':

> 'Who opposeth and exalteth himself
> above all that is called God,
> or that is worshipped;
> so that he as God
> sitteth in the temple of God,
> showing himself that he is God.
>
> Remember ye not,
> that, when I was yet with you,
> I told you these things?'
>
> *II Thessalonians 2:3-5.*

But who tells us? Yet can anything be more vital and important to the present day, or the world of our time? Is there anything more contemporary?

There can be no question but that these are the days of the fulfilment of the end prophecies. The days of the fulfilment of this word of the apostle Paul. The days in which the powers of spiritual wickedness, of false light and blinding delusion, head up their strength to promote the rise of that world ruler who most enshrines the tactics and ambitions of the Adversary.

Tactics and ambitions which may be summed up under this one grand strategy: world dominion. A strategy that God will not permit to be effectual, save at his own will, and save that it accords with his own broad providential purposes throughout the present era.

It is this that is seen unfolding in the history of the nations over the age-long period of the Old Testament. This is what lies hidden beneath the imagery and symbolism of the mysterious prophecies of Daniel. And it is what is taken up from that prophet — together with other vivid and graphic prophecies — in the culminating spiritual visions and mystical figures found in the book of the Revelation of Jesus Christ.

Particularly is this true of the seventeenth and eighteenth chapters of that book. Here is a picture, drawn in the strongest imagery, of the idea of 'Babylon'.

Not the literal place, of course; it is a question of that system of which ancient Babylon was the classic example. Not the city, but the way of life in that city. Not the actual location, but what was exemplified as to the manner of life in that location.

'Babylon' represents that form of organisation, of commerce, trade, art, pleasure. That environment of civilisation, sophistication, gratification, essential to the very idea of 'City': intrinsic to the whole conception of 'The World'.

That is what is being conveyed by the name Babylon. That is the idea. The idea of the congregation of mankind: a city.

This is depicted in two ways.

Broadly speaking, Revelation chapter seventeen mystically depicts the city as a woman. Although at first this figure must appear fantastic, once understood it is not so. Such symbolism is not without precise reasons.

Again, broadly speaking, from the end of the seventeenth chapter and through chapter eighteen, we see the revelation of the woman as a city.

So that both ideas are embodied. Both are given the one name, Babylon. First, the city as a woman; next the woman as a city.

The 'Babylon' of Revelation chapters 17 and 18 therefore does not point to some geographical situation. That is obvious. Any more than the figure could possibly refer to an actual woman. That is ridiculous. It is not literally a city nor actually a harlot.

But in these two figures are contained the principles upon which humanity can and will be unified. Those ideas of the world for which man and mankind long and aspire. But they are not of God. They are against God.

Then there is the idea of continuity.

Here is a picture of the world, 'Babylon'. Irrespective of any one particular period. This is what the world is like. At any time.

Here you have humanity, not in terms of the individual, or in local townships, or in the cities which dot a province, or even the entire country or a group of countries. It is humanity viewed from afar off, as seen from heaven: from eternity.

It is mankind as an entity. Not at a point in time: throughout time. This is how men live together, congregate the one with the other, how the world is organised. Civilised.

Time is taken account of under only one circumstance. That is, when the conditions are such that world dominion has actually been achieved or will be achieved, as a present reality. Such rare global instances in the whole of time receive special attention and are given very particular symbols.

'And here is the mind which hath wisdom.
The seven heads are seven mountains,
on which the woman sitteth.
And there are seven kings:
five are fallen,
and one is,
and the other is not yet come.
And when he cometh,
he must continue a short space.'

*Revelation 17:9,10.*

Perhaps I should say here that I quite appreciate the mystery that surrounds these verses; indeed, that pervades the entire book of the Revelation of Jesus Christ.

Hence the fact that I do not deal with the surrounding mysteries may give rise to an objection about my commenting on only a verse or two out of the midst of such obscure passages. It may be objected that my too-brief remarks about the city and harlot Babylon are inadequate as an introduction, if I wish to come particularly to a verse in that context.

I agree. Such an objection is valid. Not only do I accept it but I support it. Especially because this is the most difficult to interpret of all books, requiring the clearest calling, the longest study, the strictest discipline, the most rigorous principles, the most arduous prayer, the deepest spiritual exercise, and the most lucid clarity in the result, plain and open for all to read and judge.

I accept this as being no more than just and equal. And who is sufficient for these things? But I trust our sufficiency is of God. For having received somewhat from the Lord on the Revelation of Jesus Christ, and submitting to the disciplines mentioned, I hope that God will permit us to publish abroad the result of these labours.

But time and space fail me to do so now. Then I trust that I may be allowed to make my brief remarks from Revelation 17:9,10 at the moment, and publish the whole work at large later. Meanwhile giving assurance to the reader that any short comments on a particular text are not arbitrary, but rather taken from prolonged and strict care and study over the whole book of the Revelation.

If God will, and this is published in the future, then it will soon appear from the entire exposition, that my particular remarks here upon chapter 17:9,10 are by no means disagreeable to the context, nor counter to the tenor of the whole volume of the Revelation of Jesus Christ. Meantime if the reader carefully examines my comments against the actual verses, I think that he will find nothing contrary to the word of God.

Granted then, that the book of the Revelation is unique in the New Testament. Given that to enlarge upon any one part — in the nature of the whole — should entail an outline of the complete work. Accepted that the use of imagery is such that unless subjected to the principles of interpretation common to the whole book, it will allow every fanciful fellow untold latitude to 'prove' the wildest theories from isolated passages. Therefore I have considered it not only courteous but necessary to explain my simplified and inadequate introduction to chapter 17:9,10.

Now I come to the relevant place without further delay, resuming continuity upon the present subject: World Dominion. I repeat,

> 'There are seven kings:
> five are fallen,
> and one is,
> and the other is not yet come.'

*Revelation 17:10.*

Clearly these kings are associated with that sweeping movement of revelation which exposes in vivid imagery both the prince of this world, his agencies, and his strategy.

Satan, the prince of this world, is portrayed in that image which, were he visible and tangible, would be the appropriate form of appearance to his invisible and intangible malevolence. But he has no image at all. Then let the reader understand from this imaginative description, just how terrible is this enemy, and not least because he is spiritual and unseen.

The powers or agencies of Satan likewise. These absolutely grotesque and hideous figures arise like nightmares from the pages of the book. But they are not at all the product of wild or feverish imagination. Here are sober, careful, and rational descriptions of the equivalent in solid form of the immaterial and supernatural forces ranged against Messiah and the promises peculiar to him.

In terrifying physical terms we are given the picture of

that which can never be seen, but which is actually — did men but realise it — far more dreadful and deadly than anything viewed with the eye, or conceived by the natural mind.

The agencies of 'The great red dragon, that old serpent, called the diabolos, and Satan' are seen, first in terms of two fabled and monstrous beasts, next as the harlot and city of Babylon, and finally as that false prophet who serves the satanic interest so faithfully and well.

All mythical figures. Nevertheless they clothe with soberly chosen words and seriously considered images, the invisible and intangible enemies that fill this world and are determined upon a course that will drown it in perdition.

Now the seven kings.

These powers and agencies are their origin.

No question about that. Ranging back through the swiftly changing and kaleidoscopic imagery of these verses, first the seven kings are manifest as seven mountains on which the woman sitteth, Revelation 17:9. Meaning that the kings appear as those over whom the 'woman' has supremacy.

Once more, verse nine, there is a bewildering change of figure: the same seven mountains are seen as seven heads. What heads are these? In verse three, these heads are part of the composite picture of the first 'beast', Satan's primary agent.

Then the kings are an integral part of that agency. This demonstrates that the kings stand directly in the power and under the authority of Satan and his agencies.

# The Son of God

By these kings that old serpent, called the devil and Satan, leads the people and nations captive at his will. So? Then have they been led only six times thus far, with one yet to come? Certainly not. They are perpetually captive at his will. Then what? Then by his will in this place we are to understand not what he wants, not simply the strategy, but the times that he has virtually attained to what he wants. The actual achievement. This is what the kings represent.

If so, then occasions of world dominion.

However, the kings are numbered specifically,

> 'There are seven kings:
> five are fallen,
> and one is,
> and the other is not yet come.'

Then precisely who are these kings? Five were in the past. One was contemporary with John. And one was in the future. So that at this present time, today,

> Six are fallen,
> and the other
> is not yet come.

But he cannot be far away.

However, let us return to the conditions that obtained when John wrote. Then,

> 'Five were fallen,
> and one is,
> and the other is not yet come.'

First, who were the five which had fallen, those whom John puts in the past tense?

And where shall we look for them? We should look for them in the Old Testament. And we should look for them in terms of world dominion. That is, the kind of world dominion of which the Old Testament takes cognisance; one that regards Israel as the centre of divine activity on earth. So that we are looking for dominion over the world as known to Israel.

Then what five kings and nations had successively exercised dominion over the known world during the history of God's people Israel, and were therefore relevant to that people?

The first was Egypt.

This was the world power at the beginning of Israel, and the pharaohs attained to a vast civilisation with tributaries involving the whole habitable earth. Of this kingdom came that Pharaoh who greatly withstood Moses, whose heart the Lord hardened, and who perished in the Red Sea.

Not since the world began had there been any kingdom like unto this kingdom, no, neither for power, riches, glory nor dominion. This king was the first, and he greatly troubled Israel.

The next was the king of Assyria.

There were of course many kingdoms between Egypt and Assyria, but not in terms of world dominion. For this, only these two great nations qualified. And nearly attained, too, as regards the known world of the Old Testament.

This was that Assyria and Shalmaneser was the king, who broke up the ten tribes of Israel scattering them afar, the meanwhile populating Samaria with a strange uncircumcised people who had not known the Lord. This was the second king. He also greatly vexed Israel.

The third king was the king of Babylon.

Assyria had fallen, and the empire broken up. The Egyptians had been defeated at Carchemish. The Babylonian dominion rose to dizzy heights, an extended civilisation reaching to the bounds of the habitable earth in its conquests.

Under Nebuchadnezzar king of Babylon, Judah collapsed, Jerusalem fell, the last two tribes were carried away captive, and the last king had his eyes put out immediately after the final sight of his sons being slain. Babylon carried away the remnant of Judah and Benjamin. Nebuchadnezzar was the third king. He brought down sore lamentation upon Jerusalem.

The fourth was Persia.

The Persians defeated the Babylonians, killing Belshazzar their king. Cyrus king of Persia, and his son, established the Persian empire, but it was under Darius the Great that the dominion waxed mightily, covering the world with the greatness of the king's achievements.

Under the Persian ruler the Jews returned from captivity, and, following this felicity, were left at peace to rebuild the altar, the temple, and the walls of Jerusalem. Darius the Great was occupied with weighty matters of world conquest all over the known world. World dominion was his preoccupation. However, unlike the others, the fourth king was for the good of Jerusalem.

The fifth kingdom was Greece.

'And now will I show thee the truth. Behold, there shall stand up yet three kings in Persia; and the fourth shall be far richer than they all: and by his strength through his riches he shall stir up all against the realm of Grecia. And a mighty king shall stand up, that shall rule with great dominion, and do according to his will. And when he shall stand up, his kingdom shall be broken, and shall be divided toward the four winds of heaven.' Daniel 11:2,3,4.

This last is Alexander the Great of Macedonia, whose conquests were swift and furious, striking terror into the hearts of all the nations round about. But no sooner had he stood up to conquer the world, that in the process of so doing he fell sick and died. The Jews were delivered from the ravages of this the fifth king.

Now, these are the five kings of whom we read,

'five are fallen.'

And by these that old serpent called the diabolos and Satan, leading about the captive peoples and nations at his own will, was permitted to exert his power.

Five times, respectively, by the man whom he exalted, world dominion was at his fingertips. It was as if he whispered to each in turn as he showed him all the kingdoms of the world in a moment of time,

'All this power will I give thee, and the glory of them:

for that is delivered unto me;
and to whomsoever I will I give it.

'If thou therefore wilt worship me,
all shall be thine.'

And they did, each in his turn; they did worship him. But his promise was no good; he broke it; what he promised was never theirs. It did not come true. They were defeated, and they died. Well, what did they expect from the father of lies? Truth?

So all these five fell: Egypt, Assyria, Babylon, Persia and Greece. These are the five that were already in the past tense when the New Testament was written. 'Five are fallen.'

'And one is.'

Here is a dominion that existed at the time during which the book of the Revelation was written. Here is the king, the sixth king, with whom the apostle John was contemporary.

The sixth is Rome, under the Caesars.

Rising with massive certainty, annexing Syria, Greece, Egypt, Samaria, Judea. One after the other, subduing the nations as the Roman war machine rolled with inexorable discipline over the face of the earth.

Here was a conqueror the like of which the world had never seen. Reaching to Spain, Africa, France, Germany, Asia, England, even as far as towards the borders of India, the marching legions conquered all and nothing could withstand them.

Ruler of all the world, the whole civilised earth, all that spread from that theatre of heaven's interest, Israel still, this was the crucial kingdom and he was the paramount king.

'And one is.'

Under Caesar's rule of all the habitable earth, Jesus of Nazareth was born King of the Jews. Of this, Caesar was oblivious. Under the Roman dominion the kingdom of God was preached. But this was unknown to the world power. Under the sixth king, world dominion extended throughout the civilised earth, and an unheard voice recorded, 'My kingdom is not of this world.'

Under Caesar's all-conquering sway, the Son of God came of the seed of David to Israel, was crucified, died, and was buried. He rose the third day, was seen alive forty days of chosen witnesses, ascended into the heavens, sent the Holy Ghost from heaven, and began the inward rule of that interior kingdom of which the world and worldly Christendom was and is utterly ignorant. Because 'The kingdom of God is within you.'

Meanwhile, the balance of heaven's interest shifted from Israel. Not to the church, as those 'authorities' who have taken over the church from the Holy Ghost fondly suppose, but to the Son of God in heaven.

Wrath came upon Israel to the uttermost. Caesar destroyed Jerusalem, slew vast numbers of Jews and blasted the remainder to the four winds. Thus he strengthened the power of his world dominion on every hand.

But he fell.

Rome was burned, sacked, and conquered. The barbarians from the east swarmed in their hordes over the ordered civilisation and into the fair cities of the west. Step by step the legions retreated. Armies were withdrawn. Collapse was imminent. The long night fell over Europe. And the apostles having fallen asleep, darkness overtook the slumbering church that remained, so soon sunk into the oblivion of apostasy.

'But one is to come.'

And for nineteen hundred years, although with an undefined longing, this one has been awaited, this hope of all the world, this dream of the whole earth. Even until this present time his coming remains the elusive but increasingly vociferous demand of the rulers of all the nations, of all the peoples.

The world sees such a dominion as the solution to the mounting dilemma of all the earth. The final solution of the world problem.

As never before, the nations and kingdoms about to enter the twenty-first century, the world poised on the threshold of the year 2000 A.D., I say, as never before, the whole earth cries for a deliverer, a governor, another king of all the earth.

And as never before, organisation, communication, totalitarian control, blanket exposure, and complete integration, render the individual whether person or nation, the hapless dependant of the system. And the system, of some leader as yet undefined.

Truly, all things are now ready.

The façade that finally cracked in 1914-18. The aftermath. The pulverising repetition of 1939-45. So short an intervening period filled with discoveries and inventions beyond the wildest imagination of all mankind since the foundation of the world. That aftermath.

The decline of the twin institutional pillars of monarchy and the state church. The deceptive renaissance of earthly Israel. The collapse and decay of Protestantism. The fall of nonconformity. The ruinous failure of the Brethren movement.

The rise of atheistic socialism. The dismissal of the four fears: the fear of poverty, the fear of authority, the fear of shame, and the fear of God. The collapse of old restraints. The spread of wealth. The dissolution of morality. The undermining of money. The breakdown of distinction between male and female, young and old, married and unmarried, rich and poor, parents and children, the ruler and the ruled, one nation and another.

Unprecedented! Astonishing. No world or age could survive this disintegration of every structure, shattering of all the pillars, uprooting of every foundation, without utter disorientation. And all this within living memory. And with what effect? The world must and will cry in anguish for leadership and security.

These monumental changes are sure heralds of massive switches and movements of power in the unseen realms. They are the physical reverberations of profound realignments and final dispositions for the great climax of age-long heavenly warfare. And these staggering changes — it cannot be overstressed — are within the living memory of the aged amongst us.

I say therefore that these staggering earthly repercussions are clearly consequent upon the removal of that which 'withholdeth that he might be revealed in his time.' They are changes which appear as the harbingers of the end. This is the taking away of the hindrance: 'he who now letteth will let, until he be taken out of the way.' 'Then shall that Wicked be revealed.'

So near, these times. These are the days — everything bespeaks it — when after all the stability of ages and generations having been broken up, then occurs the saying, 'After that, he, Satan, must be loosed a little season.'

It is the time when 'Satan shall be loosed out of his prison, and shall go out to deceive the nations.' Soon now arrive the days in which that word shall be fulfilled: 'Woe to the inhabiters of the earth and of the sea! For the diabolos is come down unto you, having great wrath, because he knoweth that he hath but a short time.'

And in these days, and in the times of this deception and that wrath, shall come to pass what is written,

'But one is to come.'

Nevertheless, even until now, not yet come. Still, there is no doubt but that he is at hand, even at the doors.

Egypt. Assyria. Babylon. Persia. Greece. Rome. And the last is the greatest, the coming world ruler. The 'king' who shall come in his times.

These seven kingdoms, they appear like vast mountains. 'The seven heads are seven mountains.' Mountains rearing uniquely over the plains of history, soaring aloft the mists of time, thrusting upwards above all the unformed mass below. Seven kings.

The last is near. He is the sevenfold perfection, the personification of every ideal, of all that is of man and the world. He is the culmination of all that was sought after, the embodiment of every aspiration, the epitome of all that variously inspired the quest of each of his predecessors.

As none of those that went before, he will appear as the world's messiah, as an angel of light for deliverance, as the bright focus of every human and national loyalty.

The last is the greatest. The final and climactic struggle of the ancient Adversary for world dominion. In a manner unprecedented, all his powers and forces are released. The first 'beast'. The second 'beast'. The 'harlot city'. The 'false prophet'. All these agencies are employed in an almost overwhelming *tour de force*, a brilliant display that shall carry away all the world as one man.

In a way that is unique in history, Satan will employ the first of his agencies. For when that 'great red dragon, called the devil, and Satan' finally casts the lot for world dominion, then shall the 'beast' ascend for the last time.

Loosed for a little season, then shall the 'dragon' exert his utmost deception, his last potential, all his strength, 'for he knoweth that he hath but a short time.'

Then shall the people 'worship the beast', that is, they shall lean with glad dependence upon the state or secular power and authority. They shall rely wholly upon the world system which takes over all responsibility. With relieved gaiety they shall fall completely before such a provider, rejoicing in the prosperity, wealth, and pleasure freely brought to all people in a manner unprecedented since time began.

And not without religion. The second 'beast', with universal tolerance, gently, sweetly, dispenses love and peace. With all the accommodation of what appears in the world as the church and Christianity, there is exerted a fascination which undoubtedly revives religion. Nor is this without validity, for he 'doeth miracles' by which the authenticity of this world religion is verified, as it appears, by God himself.

Then shall pleasure prosper, and bliss seem to be universal. The nations will feel, as the seventh 'king' reigns, that the millennium of mankind has dawned at last.

But there is a minor, almost unnoticed, an infinitely small irritation to mar this blissful scene. A voice sounds aloud. A word is sent forth. A prophetic cry is raised. What impudence! Against the church? Against the world? A pathetic remnant appears to support it?

Then shall the faithful be hated with a venom that makes the hatred of Cain to pale. Unequalled since time began, with one accord, the ferocity of the whole professing church and all the world will turn against this prophetic witness — for there will be a prophetic witness — and those who dare to support it. Why should they support it? Because 'the testimony of Jesus is the spirit of prophecy.'

Unprecedented fury! Then, then, persecuted to extinction or nearly so, even of the poor remnant many falling away, then shall come days of tribulation for the faithful, the like of which has never been seen until this time. Here is the patience of the saints. And here is the delivering judgment of God. Now the end is at hand.

Then he that shall come, will come, and shall not tarry. The Lord shall come! Even so, come, Lord Jesus.

Satan shall have exerted every power and spent all the strength at his disposal, having been guided by the accumulated experience of the ages of time and the wisdom gained from precedent six times over.

Man himself and the world, now tired and disillusioned by every attempt at worldly idealism, cynical of all the tricks, trials and experiments of government for world peace, will have exhausted this the last, the greatest and the final effort.

Now nothing but disillusionment, bitterness and the stark reality so long fled, remains to be contemplated. For ever and ever.

Doomed, how Satan hates the throne of David! No wonder, so long ago, showing Jesus all the kingdoms of the world and the glory of them in a moment of time, he tempted the Heir, saying, 'All these will I give thee.' Will he? God claims the earth, and had long established that claim in the throne of David and no other, saying, To thy seed will I give it.

That Herod ruled over that throne and the land was nothing to the one born King of the Jews. Nothing. Because that figure and this world never were the issue. The seed of David was to occupy the substance not the shadow. Reign for ever not for a millennium. And rule over the reality not the figure.

'That in the dispensation of the fulness of times God might gather together in one all things in Christ, both which are in heaven, and which are on earth; even in him.'

Then cometh the kingdom. 'Thy kingdom come.' And he shall reign for ever and ever. King of kings and Lord of lords. The Lord God omnipotent reigneth.

This is that same he who was in the world these two thousand years past:

'He was in the world,
and the world was made by him,
and the world knew him not.
He came unto his own,
and his own received him not.'

On the contrary, they bayed like the hounds, 'We will not have this man to reign over us.' And they whispered like the serpent, 'We have no king but Caesar.'

This same Jesus is he whom the Jews delivered up to the Gentiles, for to be crucified. They cried with one accord, they cried 'Crucify him, crucify him.'

And Pilate wrote a title and put it on the cross. So doing he summed up the whole world, led away of Satan through divers lusts, pleasures and passions, carnal and spiritual. He summed up the world which had no room for the Son of God made of the seed of David according to the flesh, the heir come for his own.

So doing, Pilate summed up all the estates of man, for he wrote the superscription in Hebrew, Greek, and Latin, the languages of the estates.

He wrote in Hebrew.

This was the language of Israel, of religious man, the language in which the law was given, and the scriptures were written. But under its characters they crucified him. Pharisee and Sadducee, doctor and scribe, priest and scholar, they crucified him. Now, this answers to the 'second beast and the false prophet'. And the dead letter.

He wrote in Greek.

Here is the language of the great philosophers: Socrates, Plato, Aristotle. The great scientists: Pythagoras, Euclid, Archimedes, Hippocrates. The language of political philosophy, world wisdom, medicine, science, art and beauty.

'The Greeks seek after wisdom.' But, 'The world by wisdom knew not God.' No, for under the language of wisdom, the world crucified the Lord of glory. This answers to 'that old serpent, called the devil and Satan,' which 'hath deceived the whole world' by 'the lust of the flesh, the lust of the eyes, and the pride of life.'

Pilate wrote in Latin.

This was the language of the world power. The language of Caesar and the great Roman empire. This was that tongue in which the world was ruled, world dominion was established, and the kingdoms of the civilised earth were governed.

This was the tongue synonymous with order, peace and

prosperity, with all the might and glory of Rome upholding the commonwealth of the nations. But Jesus died under the Roman tongue. This answers to the 'first beast'. All the world wondered after the beast.

These are things that we are to understand. Luke tells us, 'And a superscription also was written over him in letters of Greek, and Latin, and Hebrew.' Luke — and so Paul — emphasises it: not just a superscription. There is emphasis.

A superscription 'written'. 'In letters'. No question but that the Holy Ghost stresses the writing of the letters. And from which different tongues the letters were formed. Mark where they are, and where he is in relation to them. 'Written over him in letters.'

Letters that accused him. Went over his head. Were the condemnation, the cause of his death.

Letters which signified spiritually the states: The 'second beast', the religion of this world with its ministry of the letter, the 'false prophet'. 'The old serpent', old as the garden, which deceiveth the whole world, the god of this world. The 'first beast', then, the might of Rome, but as a state, the world power, the earthly government, the politic of this world.

Under these estates the world brought the Lord of glory to be crucified in weakness.

Now these things are an allegory and answer to that which we have spoken.

Mark this well, then, for it speaks of this world in its abiding conditions. And it speaks of all that is in this world.

Also it speaks of the place of Christ Jesus in relation to the world:

'And Pilate wrote a title,
and put it on the cross.
And the writing was:

ישוע־דמן נצרת מלכא־דיהודיא

JESVS·NAZARENVS·REX·JVDAEORVM

IHCOYC·O·NAZOPAIOC·O·BACIΛEYC·TΩN·JOYΔAIΩN

'This title then read many of the Jews.'

And well they might, and might now, and all mankind, and the whole world besides, for it is significant enough.

'For the place where Jesus was crucified
was nigh to the city.'

Which thing is an allegory; for this also has a spiritual meaning. Will anyone deny it, and say that I go too far, that this is too fanciful? Let them first hear with the ear, and then judge:

'the great city,
which spiritually is called Sodom and Egypt,
where also our Lord was crucified.'

*Revelation 11:8.*

241

He that hath an ear, let him hear what the Spirit saith.

Here the context is one in which the voices of the prophets sound continually, warning the world, testifying of coming destruction. In the end of time this witness is put to death, quenched, now utterly silenced. The dead bodies of the 'two witnesses' lie in the street.

And do they cry, 'Where is the prophetic word?' No, they rejoice. They send each other presents. They dance in the streets. But not for long, for the Spirit of life from God shall raise up his witness again, and none shall let it.

However, for the present, observe that Revelation 11:8 shows that Babylon the great — in the last days, mind — answers to Sodom in Abraham's day, and to Egypt at the time of Moses. Not that Egypt was a city, incidentally. And both answer to the

> 'place where Jesus was crucified
> nigh to the city,'
> *John 19:20.*

for it is written, after that Babylon had been called Sodom and Egypt:

> 'where also
> our Lord was crucified.'
>
> *Revelation 11:8.*

So the meaning is spiritual. 'Nigh to the city' is spiritual. It is the world city. The city at once Babylon, the country Egypt, the place Sodom. These all merge together with Jerusalem below, having the tongue of the Hebrew, the Greek and the Roman.

The world as a state. The world city regarded as
continuously inhabited and acting without any break from
generation to generation or nation to nation. It is how
the world acts as a social unit. As a city. Irrespective of
barriers. Such as which generation or which tongue. Hence:

> 'nigh to the city:
> it was written
> in Hebrew,
> and Greek,
> and Latin.'

> *John 19:20.*

Crucified, this king, by the world. 'We will not have this
man to reign over us.' No, for even as to the poor figure of
the throne in Canaan, man did his utmost to overturn it,
when he hung the King of the Jews on the tree.

Three days later, forty days later, and fifty days later,
there came to pass what is written:

> 'He that sitteth in the heavens
> shall laugh:
> the LORD shall have them
> in derision.'

Why? They had overturned David's throne. Then why
did God laugh?

Because it was only a type! That was their laughable
mistake. And they made it. And God laughed.

Like fools they blundered in the dead letter, and missed

the spiritual meaning entirely. And the derision of heaven
floated down upon the wind.

'He that sitteth in the heavens shall laugh:
the LORD shall have them in derision.'

It was but a type! The meanwhile,

'Yet
have I set my king
upon my holy hill of Zion.'

Yet. Regard the 'yet'.

Yet he is ascended to the throne of glory above all
heavens, as we have before shown. Yet. Yet he reigns
within. But then what?

Then, at the end of the age, when time shall be no more,
after Satan's last permitted attempt in the will of men and
consent of the nations, to establish world dominion, peace
and goodwill towards all mankind, with the welfare of the
state and the blessing of religion: then cometh the end.

Then the 'yet' shall be no more. It will have finished.

Then comes the relief of the few remaining persecuted
disciples, the poor scattered saints, the hounded remnant,
already long at their wits' end. Branded as fanatics,
bigoted, mad, antisocial, unreasonable, and at last really
unchristian, best put away for the good of an otherwise
universal harmony. Then they shall have relief.

Then it will come. The end shall come. 'Yet' will be
ended.

## and Seed of David

'And I saw heaven opened,
and behold a white horse;
and he that sat upon him was called
Faithful and True,
and in righteousness he doth judge
and make war.
His eyes were as a flame of fire,
and on his head were
MANY CROWNS;
and he had a name written, that no man knew,
but he himself.
And he was clothed with a vesture
dipped in blood:
and his name is called THE WORD OF GOD.
And the armies
which were in heaven
followed him upon white horses,
clothed in fine linen,
white and clean.
And out of his mouth goeth a sharp sword,
that with it he should smite the nations:
and he shall rule them with a rod of iron:
and he treadeth
the winepress of the fierceness and wrath
of Almighty God.
And he hath on his vesture and on his thigh
a name written,
KING OF KINGS, AND LORD OF LORDS.'


This is the seed of David. This is the Son of God made
of the seed of David according to the flesh.

This is the humiliated servant. This is that Jesus whom
they crucified. This is Jesus of Nazareth, the King of the

Jews. Now the dead are raised to judgment. Now the saints are vindicated in glory.

But will the world remember? Yes. 'For they shall look on him whom they have pierced.' They will remember. 'And all kindreds of the earth shall wail because of him. Even so. Amen.'

And now he cometh to judgment, to judge the world in righteousness, to raise the dead, to justify the saints, to damn the sinners, to bring the world to a melting fire, to dissolve the earth in molten heat, to roll up the heavens as a scroll, to divide between heaven and hell, to bring in the holy city, the new Jerusalem, the world to come, to fulfil his kingdom at last.

> 'And the Lord God shall give unto him
> the throne of his father David:
> And he shall reign over the house of Jacob
> for ever;
> and of his kingdom
> there shall be no end.'

How could there be an end? In the everlasting resurrection of eternity? In the world to come in perpetuity? Here, there is no end, world without end. Amen.

Now, this is the Son of God. This is the seed of David.

This is the king.

The absolute king. King of kings. And Lord of lords.

★

Now then, having drawn such vital lessons from the life of David, it is easy for us to perceive why it is that the Holy Ghost by the mouth of the chosen apostles insists upon the title 'son of David'.

Writing to Gentiles otherwise ignorant of the great king of Israel from of old time, nevertheless the terms of the gospel are explicit. Then learn them. Else ignore them at your peril.

Even in no more than a bare summary of the gospel as in Romans 1:3-4, 'the seed of David' is imperative. It is *sine qua non*. The Holy Ghost by his elect vessel commands our faith that we receive with meekness the engrafted word. The word of this essential gospel truth,

> 'The Son of God,
> come of the seed of David
> according to the flesh.'

To lay hold upon this truth, to believe it, I say, with a threefold witness, this is what is meant to

> 'believe on the Lord Jesus Christ
> and be saved.'

And if, led by the Spirit, receptive to the scriptures, guided by the apostolic word, the reader firmly lays hold upon the Son of God by faith, and believes the promises as concerning the son of David, I dare say, if so, then

> 'the prayers of David the son of Jesse
> are ended.'

Yes and fulfilled too. For all these spiritual exercises
and prayers of the faithful in time past, and those who
went before, had but one desire for us who are to come in
the future:

that we might believe with faith unfeigned;

that we might be willing from a guileless heart;

that we might be found wholly following in obedience

DAVID'S SON AND DAVID'S LORD,

the Son of God, come of the seed of David according to
the flesh.

Amen and amen.

• • •

# CURRENT BOOKLIST

## Obtainable from the publishers

## TITLES:

## NOAH AND THE FLOOD                    *60p*

"Mr. Metcalfe makes a skilful use of persuasive
eloquence as he challenges the reality of one's
profession of faith ... he gives a rousing call to a
searching self-examination and evaluation of one's
spiritual experience."

*The Monthly Record of the Free Church of Scotland.*

"In an age which claims to put the practical accent on
Christian interpretation of scripture, it is refreshing
to go back and look at the spiritual meaning in the
Bible. We need some forceful reminder that refuge
may be found in the Ark."

*The Catholic Fireside.*

"Noah and the Flood is an excellent exposition of
the story of Noah found in Genesis chapters 6-9.
No one reading this book can fail to be stirred by the
author's challenging and heart-searching exposition."

*Dr. A. J. Monty White.*

"Many will appreciate the original thought and
clarity of expression and the application to the
individual today."

*Dr. F. Tatford (Prophetic Witness).*

252

## DIVINE FOOTSTEPS                    *40p*

Divine Footsteps traces the pathway of the feet of
the Lord the Son of man from the very beginning in
the prophetic figures of the true in the Old Testament
through the reality in the New; doing so in a way of
experimental spirituality. At the last a glimpse of the
coming glory is beheld as his feet are viewed as
standing at the latter day upon the earth.

*"Originality of thought and approach is apparent."*

*The Expository Times.*


## THE RED HEIFER                      *25p*

This book has been edited from a powerful sermon
preached by John Metcalfe in Tylers Green Chapel.
The verbal directness makes the book very readable
and simple to understand.

The Red Heifer was the name given to a sacrifice
used by the children of Israel in the Old Testament
— as recorded in Numbers chapter 19 — in which a
heifer was slain and burned. Cedar wood, hyssop and
scarlet were cast into the burning, and the ashes
were mingled with running water and put in a vessel.
It was kept for the children of Israel for a water of
separation: it was a purification for sin.

In this unusual book the sacrifice is brought up to
date and its relevance to the church today is shown.


255

## THE WELLS OF SALVATION                    *60p*

The Wells of Salvation is written from a series of
seven powerful addresses preached at Tylers Green
Chapel. It is a forthright and experimental exposition
of Isaiah 12:3, 'Therefore with joy shall ye draw
water out of the wells of salvation.'

We quote:

John Metcalfe, acknowledged to be 'perhaps the most
gifted expositor and powerful preacher of our day'
nonetheless possesses a controversial challenge in his
ministry which presses home long-ignored issues in a
way 'which cannot be ignored'.

This is to be seen clearly in The Wells of Salvation,
in and of itself a unique and richly rewarding study
worthy of the reader's careful attention.


"Among truly great Christian works."

*Methodist review.*


"Outstanding."

*The English Churchman.*


"Impressive."

*The Life of Faith.*

# TRACTS:

257

## THE TWO PRAYERS OF ELIJAH                    *10p*

This tract, first printed in 1972, was reprinted in 1975.
It shows the spiritual significance of the drought, the
cloudburst, and the two prayers of Elijah.


## THE GOSPEL OF GOD                    *stiff cover,  25p*
### Tract for the Times 1

Beautifully designed, this tract positively describes the
gospel under the following headings: The Gospel is of God;
The Gospel is Entirely of God; The Gospel is Entire in
Itself; The Gospel is Preached; The Gospel Imparts Christ;
and, Nothing But the Gospel Imparts Christ. The last two
headings also expose the recent moves to undermine the
truth that Christ is conveyed simply through the gospel.

"It takes the discernment of an utterly fearless man like
John Metcalfe to tear the mask off the moves that are
taking place in the high circles of the church today. Here
are 48 pages of verbal dynamite exposing the way in which
the evangelical faith is being undermined by the statements
of the Anglican-Roman Catholic Commission in its
pronouncements concerning the meaning of the eucharist,
the priestly and sacrificial character of the ministry, and
papal authority."

*From the comment of a Methodist minister.*


## THE STRAIT GATE                    *stiff cover,  25p*
### Tract for the Times 2

Exceptionally well made, this booklet consists of extracts
from 'The Messiah', compiled in such a way as to challenge
the shallowness of much of today's 'easy-believism', whilst
positively pointing to the strait gate.

*STOP PRESS ANNOUNCEMENT*

**Eternal Sonship and Taylor Brethren**
Tract for the Times No. 3
Price 25p

has now been published,

45 pages, with special stiff gloss finished cover featured in
this high quality series.

This booklet is highly recommended, particularly for those
perplexed by James Taylor's teaching against the eternal
sonship of Christ.

This teaching impugns the doctrine of J.N. Darby and his
colleagues, denies the teaching of the Reformation, and
refuses the orthodox preaching of the person of Christ
throughout the ages. Besides this it recants upon the earlier
ministry of Taylor himself. Above all, James Taylor's latter
teaching against the eternal sonship of Christ contradicts
the faith once delivered to the saints, and defies the
apostles' doctrine, denying what has always been held
about the eternity of Father, Son and Holy Ghost.

In a day when the term 'believer' is used so lightly that the
vast majority think of it as barely related to *what* one
believes — although in fact what one believes gives the only
true title to the term 'believer' — this Tract for the Times
thoroughly searches out truth from error, the believer from
the infidel, the true Christ from the false, and leaves the
reader in no doubt whatsoever as to the issue.

## 'APOSTOLIC FOUNDATION
## OF THE CHRISTIAN CHURCH':

259

## FOUNDATIONS UNCOVERED

*30p*

**Volume 1**

Foundations Uncovered is a small book of some
37 pages. This is the Introduction to the major
series: 'The Apostolic Foundation of the Christian
Church'.

Rich in truth, the Introduction deals comprehensively
with the foundation of the apostolic faith under the
descriptive titles: The Word, The Doctrine, The
Truth, The Gospel, The Faith, The New Testament,
and The Foundation.

The contents of the book reveal: The Fact of the
Foundation; The Foundation Uncovered; What the
Foundation is not; How the Foundation is Described;
and, Being Built upon the Foundation.

*Our reviewer states:*

"This book comes with the freshness of a new
Reformation.

"In this Introduction, the author sets out the
exhaustive method of arriving at the knowledge of
the apostolic doctrine of the Christian faith.

"He outlines that objective body of truth which sets
forth the Son of God, and which is the only valid
foundation on which the church is built."

## THE BIRTH OF JESUS CHRIST
**Volume 2**

45p

"The author expresses with great clarity the truths revealed to him in his study of holy scripture at depth. We are presented here with a totally lofty view of the Incarnation.

"This is a fascinating and enlightening study. The author's examination of Biblical material is the reverent approach of someone who recognises the living quality of God's Word, and who waits to be instructed from it without pre-determining his own attitude.

"The very spirit of adoration and worship rings through these pages. In this new section of his work 'The Apostolic Foundation of the Christian Church', there is again indication that John Metcalfe is to be classed amongst the foremost expositors of our age; and although the value of his contribution to Christian thought may not yet be acclaimed, his writings have about them that quality of timelessness that makes me sure they will one day take their place among the heritage of truly great Christian works."

*From a review by Rev. David Catterson.*

"A book to be studied ... an outstanding contribution."

*The English Churchman.*

"Uncompromisingly faithful to scripture ... has much to offer which is worth serious consideration ... deeply moving."

*The Expository Times.*

"A thoroughly orthodox outlook ... impressive."

*The Life of Faith.*

261

## THE MESSIAH
### Volume 3

£1.20

"This is no ordinary book. It is extraordinary, judged by the standards of godly doctrine in any age, and especially so when compared to the comparative impoverishment of the modern pulpit and pen. I firmly believe that it will be treasured as a spiritual classic by people not yet born.

"It draws out the inwardness of the beatitudes in a truly experimental way. It faithfully warns of judgment to come; with alarming descriptions of the Great Day. Law and gospel are distinguished, yet both honoured. Outstanding are the passages dealing with the threefold temptation of Jesus; and the Baptist's threefold description of the Messiah's work. What glorious light breaks out of the saying, 'Suffer it to be so now: for thus it becometh us to fulfil all righteousness.'

"It bears throughout the stamp of true ministry, raised up of GOD, not in letter but touching the spirit, bearing life. It comes from one who has been on his face, eaten the roll, and spoken only after sitting down seven days, (Ezekiel ch. 3) and the LORD'S people, whether they will hear or whether they will forbear (for they are a rebellious people) yet shall know that there hath been a prophet among them."

*David Hughes, B.Sc., M.B., Ch.B.*

"Its author is clearly a great lover of the Bible."

*Maurice Nassan S.J., Catholic Herald.*

"Something of the fire of the ancient Hebrew prophet ... Metcalfe has spiritual and expository potentials of a high order."

*The Life of Faith.*

262

# ORDER FORM

|                                          |           |       | Quantity |
|------------------------------------------|-----------|-------|----------|
| Noah and the Flood . . . . . . . . . . . . . . . | 60p   | + *19p* | ☐ |
| Divine Footsteps . . . . . . . . . . . . . . . . | 40p   | + *12p* | ☐ |
| The Red Heifer . . . . . . . . . . . . . . . . | 25p   | + *12p* | ☐ |
| The Wells of Salvation . . . . . . . . . . . . | 60p   | + *26p* | ☐ |
| The Two Prayers of Elijah . . . . . . . . . . | 10p   | + *7p* | ☐ |
| The Gospel of God . . . . . . . . . . . . . . | 25p   | + *10p* | ☐ |
| The Strait Gate . . . . . . . . . . . . . . . . | 25p   | + *10p* | ☐ |
| Foundations Uncovered . . . . . . . . . . . | 30p   | + *12p* | ☐ |
| The Birth of Jesus Christ . . . . . . . . . . | 45p   | + *15p* | ☐ |
| The Messiah . . . . . . . . . . . . . . . . . . | £1.20 | + *55p* | ☐ |
| The Son of God and Seed of David . £1.10 |       | + *33p* | ☐ |

*(Figures in italics show postage & packing)* *

NAME AND ADDRESS  (in block capitals)

_____

_____

_____

Enclose remittance with order.
Cheques payable to 'The Publishing Trust'.

* *Postage costs are correct at time of going to press, and apply to the U.K. only.*